We are Indians and we understand that you
do not need our friendship. But, just as all are
equal before death, so nature itself has taught
us that human equality should exist without
discrimination. Discrimination arises from
the spirits of the gods of ambition, and of the
avarice which pits brother against brother.
For our mother, the Earth, we are one.

Arhuaco statement, Colombia

In association with
Survival International

Quadrille
PUBLISHING

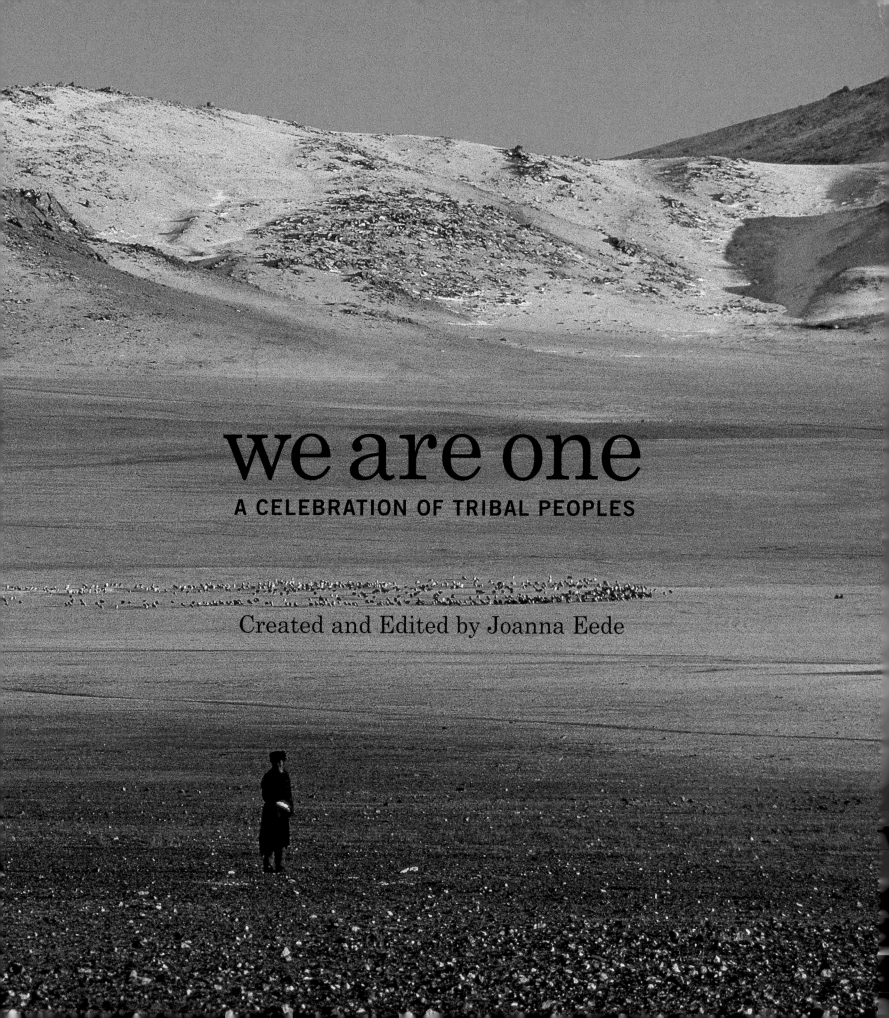

we are one

A CELEBRATION OF TRIBAL PEOPLES

Created and Edited by Joanna Eede

Foreword

Mori Kami Yamaki – We are all one. This is the essence of the book. We all share a common humanity, and we are unified by our mother, the Earth. We have different cultures and languages, yet in a much older and deeper way, we are all from one. The same spirit of life lives in us all. Without our shared ancestors, none of us would be here. We are all connected; this will never change.

My home is the rainforest in Brazil. I was born in the headwaters of the river Toototobi; today I live in Watoriki, the place we call 'mountain of the wind'. The rainforest has been the home of my people, the ancient Yanomami, for thousands of years. It is hard to describe how connected my people are to nature. We have never thought about it until now; it is just part of us, it is the blood in our veins. It nourishes us physically and spiritually; I am created by the animals and plants I have eaten and gathered, and by the breath of life that has passed through me. My skin is the colour of the Earth. It does not separate me from what is outside, it connects me to it. You can't uproot us and put us in another land; we don't exist away from the forest. We belong in it.

My Yanomami people have always lived in peace with the forest, which we share with other creatures. You can see our love of the Earth in this book. We know our Yanomami land in the same way our brothers, the Inuit, know the sea-ice of the Arctic or the Dongria Kondh people the hills of Orissa, or the Kogi Indians the snow peaks of Colombia. We know the streams and the rapids, the paths of the peccary, the call of the tapir and the song of the toucan. We understand the seasons of the peach-palm trees and the ways of the sloth and the monkeys and all animals that live high in the canopy. We know these things just as our Penan brothers of Sarawak know the migration of the wild pig and the Bushmen of Botswana the tracks of the eland. This is how we live, today. Our ancestors taught us to understand our lands and animals, we have used this knowledge carefully, for our existence depends on it.

Yet injustices have been carried out against tribal peoples all over the world for over 500 years. And they are still happening. We are removed from our lands so that governments and corporations can carry out logging and road-building and the mining that unearths gold and diamonds and other riches of the Earth. My Yanomami land was invaded by miners. The government didn't stop them and Brazilian society let it happen. A fifth of our people died from diseases we had never known, which our shamans couldn't cure. Goldminers are still working illegally in our territory, giving us malaria and polluting the rivers and forests with mercury.

We are called undeveloped because we have no electricity, and because we do not live in stone buildings or use computers. We are considered backward or stupid because we cannot read the language of books. We are called poor or primitive for having few possessions and clothes, or because we don't have cars, televisions and bank accounts. The myths of our ancestors and the wisdom of our shamanic spirits are called useless.

But we are not poor, or primitive. We are just as human as our brothers who live in cities, who learn from books and work in offices and wear expensive clothes. How can we be backward when we know how to protect the rainforest? How can we be primitive when our people live peacefully together in communities that are kind to each other, and that make us strong? How can we be stupid when our instinct is to protect, not destroy, the environment? Our wisdom is not useless. It is the wisdom of the Earth, which is very important for the survival of humanity.

The desire for possessions is destructive. Nothing that can be bought, or sold, has any real meaning. Possessions are looked upon as symbols of advanced humanity, yet they disappear with the wind. All they do is cloud the mind and pollute the soul. They're used for comfort and for pride, but they prevent people from knowing the great truths nature teaches us. They are just distractions. And they consume and destroy the Earth's resources. The Yanomami do not want, or need, possessions.

What we do need is respect. We need respect for our cultures and for our beliefs. We need respect for our rituals and our choices. We need to be listened to and treated as equals and given a say in the decisions that affect us. And we need to be able to live the lives we choose to live, not the lives other people think we should live.

The world needs to listen to the cry of the Earth, which is asking for help. It is dangerous to abuse nature. You are worried about climate change. It is arriving. The sky is full of smoke because the *napë*, the non-Indians, are logging and burning our rainforest. The rains come late, the sun behaves in a strange way. The lungs of the sky are polluted. The world is ill. We know it is happening.

We know the health of the Amazon. We know that when you destroy the rainforest, you cut the arteries of the future and the world's force just ebbs away.

So it is very important that we fight together to stop this destruction. Why is it taking so long for the world to believe that if we hurt nature, we hurt ourselves? The Earth demands a greater respect or we will all die.

In my Yanomami home, we hear the songs of different Amazonian birds. We hear the song of the red macaw, of the parrot and of the eagle. It is the same with tribal peoples around the world. We sing with different voices, but we are singing about the same Earth. So you will read in this book some of our stories. They are beautiful stories of the seas, of the skies, about our relationships with the forests, snowfields and deserts.

I was born to fight for the rights of my Yanomami people. You, the *napë*, must help us. We are working to save our rainforest for everyone. I go out into the world to tell people this. If we join hands in our struggle, if we become as one, our united strength will help the planet. These are my words.

Davi Kopenawa Yanomami.

Davi Kopenawa, Yanomami, Brazil

LIST OF NAMED CONTRIBUTORS

A.C. Grayling, *Philosopher, UK*

Ailton Krenak, *Brazil*

Alan Campbell, *Anthropologist, UK*

Alona Yefimenko, *Even, Kamchatka, Siberia*

Amilton Lopes, *Guarani-Kaiowá, Brazil*

Arau, *Penan, Malaysia*

Arundhati Roy, *Writer, India*

Black Elk, *Oglala Sioux, USA*

Bruce Parry, *TV Presenter, Ibiza, Spain*

Carlo Petrini, *Founder, Slow Food, Italy*

Caroline Lucas, *MEP and Leader of the Green Party, UK*

Cecilia Mitchell, *Mohawk, USA*

Christopher Robbins, *Author, UK*

Claude Lévi-Strauss, *Anthropologist, France*

Colin Samson, *Sociologist and Writer, UK*

Colin Firth, *Actor, UK*

Colin Thubron, *Author, UK*

Damien Hirst, *Artist, UK*

Dan George, *Salish, USA*

Daniel Ashini, *Innu, Canada*

Daniel Everett, *Illinois State University, USA*

Daquoo Xukuri, *Bushman, Botswana*

Davi Kopenawa, *Yanomami, Brazil*

David Courchene, *Manitoba, Canada*

Dawat Lupung, *Penan, Malaysia*

Desmond Tutu, *Archbishop Emeritus, Cape Town, South Africa*

Doris Pilkington Garimara, *Aborigine, Australia*

Eduardo Galeano, *Author, Uruguay*

Evaristo Nugkuag Ikanan, *Aguaruna, Peru*

Fiona Watson, *Survival, UK*

George Monbiot, *Author, UK*

Germaine Greer, *Author, UK/Australia*

Glenn Shepard, *Goeldi Museum, Brazil*

Hayden Burgess, *Hawaii*

Hugh Brody, *Anthropologist and Filmmaker, Canada*

Jane Goodall, *Founder, the Jane Goodall Institute and UN Messenger of Peace, UK*

Jean-Marie Le Clézio, *Author, France*

Jean Pierre Ashini, *Innu, Canada*

Jerome Lewis, *Anthropologist, UK*

Joan Halifax, *Author, USA*

Joanna Eede, *Journalist, UK*

Joanna Lumley, *Actress, UK*

Jonathon Porritt, *Environmentalist and Author, UK*

José Alonso Álvarez, *Ornithologist, Peru*

Juaneco, *Asháninka, Peru*

Jumanda Gakelebone, *Gana Bushman, Botswana*

Kamalurre Mehinaku, *Xingu, Brazil*

Kari Herbert, *Author and Photographer, UK*

Kiplangat Cheruyot, *Ogiek, Kenya*

Kotsi Mmaba, *Bushman, Botswana*

Kurt Jackson, *Artist, UK*

Kxao Moses, *Juhoan Bushman, Namibia*

Lame Deer, *Lakota Sioux, USA*

Laurens van der Post, *Author, UK*

Lemeikoki Ole Ngiyaa, *Maasai, Tanzania*

Linda Hogan, *Chicksaw, USA*

Lindsay Duffield, *Survival, UK*

Luther Standing Bear, *Oglala Lakota Sioux, USA*

Malani Pai, *Pai Ohana, Solomon Islands*

Mansoram, *West Papua*

Marcos Veron, *Guarani-Kaiowá, Brazil*

Marina Silva, *Environmentalist and Politician, Brazil*

Megaron Txukarramae, *Mentuktire Kayapó, Brazil*

Mike Koostachin, *Cree, Canada*

Mogetse Kaboikanyo, *Kgalagadi, Botswana*

Molatwe Mokalake, *Gana Bushman, Botswana*

Noam Chomsky, *Author, USA*

Norma Kassi, *Gwich'in, USA*

Norman Hallendy, *Author, Canada*

Norman Lewis, *Writer, UK*

Orlando Makuxi, *Brazil*

Orlando Villas Boas, *Indian expert and founder of Xingu Park, Brazil*

Pat Dodson, *Aborigine, Australia*

Peacemaker, *founder of the Iroquois Confederacy, USA*

Peter Irniq, *Inuit, Canada*

Peter Matthiessen, *Author, USA*

Piers Vitebsky, *Anthropologist and Author, UK*

Richard Gere, *Actor, USA*

Robin Hanbury-Tenison, *President, Survival, UK*

Rosalino Oritz, *Guarani-Ñandeva, Brazil*

Roy Sesana, *Gana Bushman, Botswana*

Satish Kumar, *Author, UK*

Sheila Watt-Cloutier, *Inuit, Canada*

Sitting Bull, *Hunkpapa Sioux, USA*

Stephen Corry, *Director, Survival, UK*

Sun Bear, *Chippewa, USA*

Sydney Possuelo, *Indian expert, Co-ordinator, Uncontacted Indians Unit, FUNAI (Brazilian government Indian affairs department), Brazil*

Tony Juniper, *Environmentalist, UK*

Unga Paran, *Penan, Malaysia*

Upendra Lal Chakma, *Jumma, Bangladesh*

Vandana Shiva, *Scientist, India*

Vine Deloria Jr., *Author, USA*

Vyachslav Aukhaki, *Siberia*

Wade Davis, *Explorer in Residence, National Geographic, USA*

Wandjuk Marika, *Aborigine, Australia*

Wellington Gomes Figueiredo, *Indian expert, FUNAI , Brazil*

William Milliken, *Botanist, Royal Botanic Gardens, Kew, UK*

Xawa Gaima, *Gana Bushman, Botswana*

Xlarema Phuti, *Gana Bushman woman, Botswana*

Zac Goldsmith, *Environmentalist, UK*

Note to reader: the text that accompanies the photographs used in We Are One does not always reflect the tribal people shown in the image. The juxtaposition is intentional in order to illustrate the universal nature of some tribal beliefs and values.

CONTENTS

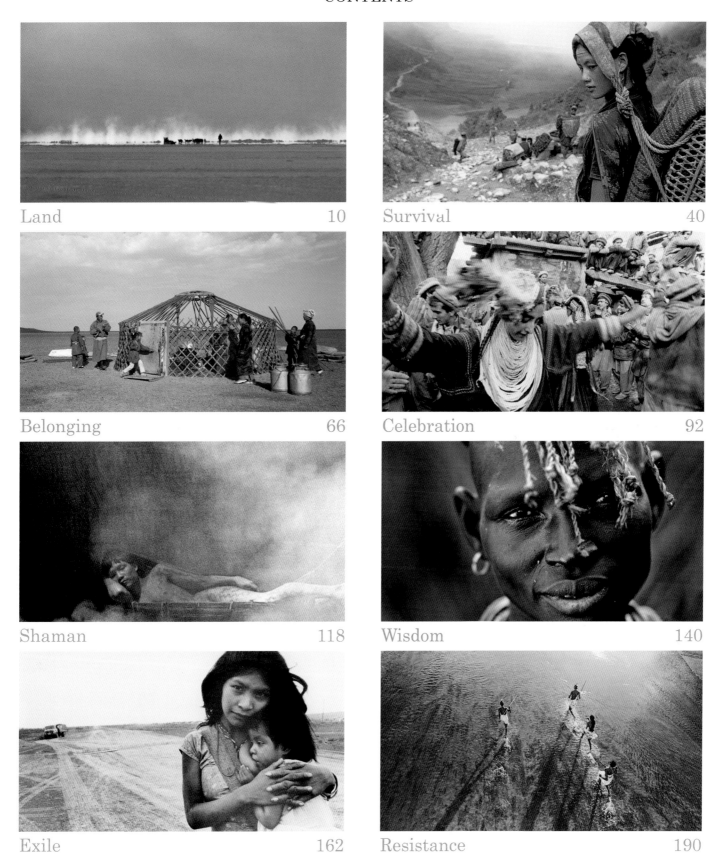

Introduction

I once returned from Amazonia to Bogotá in an old cargo plane, which also carried a handful of young Indians travelling out of the rainforest for the first time. They were unfazed by the flight, perhaps because they saw nothing untoward about the wire wrapped around the handles, securing the doors of the decrepit wartime DC-3. They were about to walk a city street for the very first time.

Once they had left the airport, their first reaction was to stop and greet everyone they passed, to touch hands and announce their names, just as they would at home. As far as they were concerned, to omit this basic greeting was unthinkable. As the crowd thronged past, muffled against the Andean cold, it took the Indians only a minute to see the impossibility of introducing themselves to everyone. They quickly buried their bewilderment in self-deprecating hilarity, but the warmth and humanity of their intention has always stayed with me.

There are 370 million indigenous people worldwide, of which 150 million are tribal; people who have developed their own ways of life for thousands of years, from the Amazon rainforest to the Siberian Arctic. Largely self-sufficient and distinct from their countries' mainstream societies in language, belief and approach to life, they include the most vulnerable minorities in the world, and are at risk of losing everything that provides their livelihood and gives their lives meaning.

Despite huge differences in culture and geography, most indigenous tribes not only share deep practical, historical and spiritual connections to their ancestral lands, but have in common the persecution they have long experienced at the hands of more dominant societies. The 21st century's technological achievements and material prosperity for a few – the hallmarks of 'progress' – are at odds with the barbaric persecution of tribal peoples that began with the European 'discovery' of the New Worlds, and has continued ever since. With superior strength and firepower, these powerful forces have appropriated tribal lands for colonisation, logging, mining, oil exploration, road building and any number of avaricious motives. They have also sought to impose their alien ways of life on societies that have thrived for millennia. In so doing, and in the false name of material and cultural 'progress', intricate and diverse peoples have been destroyed.

'If it be the part of 'civilisation' to maim, rob and thwart, then what is progress?' asked the Sioux Indian, Luther Standing Bear. The answer seems to be that 'progress' is not synonymous with ethics. It has become recognised as *the* life-enhancing truth – one that asserts that only certain societies have advanced; one so persuasive that those who live differently are considered inferior. As a consequence, they are vulnerable to abominable abuses of their human rights.

Progress, in fact, often kills. Survival International was established in 1969, following an article written by journalist Norman Lewis in *The Sunday Times* that highlighted the atrocities being inflicted on Brazilian Indians. Survival International has since worked for tribal peoples' rights to own their lands and to live in the way they choose. Forty years later, there is no doubt that the tide has shifted, however slowly, in favour of indigenous peoples. Then, massacre and disease were so commonplace that it was believed that there would be no Indians left in Brazil by the end of the century (on average, one tribe a year was made extinct in the 20th century). Thankfully, tribal issues have been pushed into the political and cultural arena, and very few people now believe that the best future lies in assimilating them into mainstream societies.

There is no room for complacency, however. There are racist barriers yet to be overcome, and many tribal peoples – both those who have contact with the outside world and those who do not – are still at risk of extinction. Similar racist forces sustained the slave trade 200 years ago but ultimately public opinion proved too strong, and slavery was outlawed. Just as it is inconceivable to think a return to the slave trade could be sanctioned, so I am sure that the power of public opinion will eventually succeed for tribal peoples.

Survival International has long sought to give tribal peoples a voice, a platform that they would not otherwise have. *We Are One* is such a platform. It portrays, in the words of tribespeople from every continent, their lives, homelands, cultures and problems, and is both a celebration and a collective call to arms. In a unique act of solidarity, their united voice is supported by beautiful and thought-provoking contributions from international supporters, writers and photographers. They entreat the world to listen to tribal peoples' wisdom and advice, and join them in the fight for their rights.

The collective format of *We Are One* also reflects a truth which tribal peoples perhaps understand better than most: that meaning in life lies in *belonging* – to each other, to our immediate surroundings, and to the world at large. In the relentless search for advancement and material progress we have perhaps alienated ourselves from our deepest human needs, which surely lie in our connections to each other and to the Earth. I fleetingly witnessed this innate appreciation of belonging when the Colombian Indians greeted strangers on a street in Bogotá.

Tribal people are the beacons that illuminate the importance of these connections. If we destroy them, we smother these lights, and so make our future far less human. I believe their survival, far from being a fringe concern, is one of the greatest humanitarian concerns of our time.

They have a right to be here and I am not alone in believing they will survive.

STEPHEN CORRY, DIRECTOR, SURVIVAL INTERNATIONAL

Land

High in the Niyamgiri Hills of Orissa, India, live the Dongria Kondh people. They call themselves *Jharnia*, the 'protectors of streams', as, for centuries, they have cared for the mineral-rich rivers that rise within the hills' lush forests. Thousands of miles away, the Pehuenche Indians of the Chilean Andes take their name from the *pehuen*, an ancient monkey puzzle tree indigenous to their lands.

For most tribal peoples, land and life are inextricably linked. Earth is the bedrock of their lives, the provider of food and shelter, the sacred burial ground of their ancestors and the spiritual focus of their lives. Importantly, it is also the inheritance of their children. Land forms the backbone of tribal cultures, moulds distinct languages and shapes the way they see the world. 'This land is where we are at home, we know its ways,' says an Akawaio woman from Guyana. The affinity with their homelands is reflected in the names tribal peoples call themselves: they are the savannah people, the people of the headwaters, the people from the wild pig place.

'Every place has a name,' says Nhari, a Bushman elder from Botswana. Their creation myths, poems and stories are rich in allusions to the beauty of their diverse habitats – tundra, sea-ice, mountains, deserts, oceans and prairies – and to the sanctity of nature. For the Guarani of Brazil, land is a precious gift from *Ñande Ru*, the great father; for the Amazonian Yanomami, home is *urihi*, a forest-land covered with the mirrors of dancing spirits; for the Oglala Sioux of the USA, land is imbued with the essence of *Wakan Tanka*, the Great Mystery. Home to Australian Aborigines is rooted in the Dreamtime, an era long past when the Earth was formed.

Most tribal peoples have lived on their lands for thousands of years. The Sentinelese, for example, are thought to have lived in the Andaman Islands for about 60,000 years. As a result, most know their territories intimately; there is, as an Innu man says, 'never an unrecognisable place'. The reindeer-herding Khanty people know the moss, lichen and larch trees of their Siberian taiga as intimately as the Dani people know the limestone outcrops of Papua's highlands. The Innu of Canada are as in tune with the rocky barrens of their homeland, *Nitassinan*, as are the Hopi people with the wind-worn mesas of their Arizona lands.

Tribal peoples typically have a holistic view of nature and see man as part of, not separate from, the Earth. To them it is a fertile, living entity that has intrinsic, not merely utilitarian value; it is not a passive, inanimate commodity to be exploited for commercial expansion and economic advancement. For the Makuxi of Guyana and Brazil, nature is imbued with a powerful energy called *stekaton,* the life force. 'It breathes, though you don't notice it,' says Davi Kopenawa Yanomami. At a time of such global ecological crises, it may be prudent to listen to their views.

Separation from their ancestral lands is, more often than not, catastrophic for tribal peoples. When control over land is lost, or when they are prevented from using it in accordance with their traditions, the long-term mental and physical health of the people suffers hugely. The late Marta Guarani from Brazil said, 'We Indians are like plants. How can we live without our soil, without our land?' Land for tribal peoples is not a pretty view, or a weekend retreat. It is their larder, their guide, their happiness – their lifeline.

We did not think of the great open plains, the beautiful rolling hills, the winding streams with tangled growth, as 'wild'. Only to the white man was nature a 'wilderness' and only to him was it 'infested' with 'wild' animals and 'savage' people. To us it was tame.

From Wakan Tanka, the Great Spirit, there came a great unifying life force that flowed in and through all things – the flowers of the plains, blowing winds, rocks, trees, birds, animals – and was the same force that had been breathed into the first man. Thus all things were kindred, and were brought together by the same Great Mystery.

Luther Standing Bear, Oglala Lakota Sioux, USA

This land keeps us
together within its
mountains – we come
to understand that we
are not just a few people
or separate villages,
but one people belonging
to a homeland.
—
Akawaio, Guyana

Often at dawn we stood still in the shallows among the rocks above the rapids armed with long, supple, blue-bush wands. When the golden bream on their way up-stream rose to the surface, a surface so filled with light of the opening sky that they might have been birds with folded wings swooping out of the blue, we would smack the water smartly over their heads just as the River Bushmen had done, and the shock would turn the fish over on their backs to drift helplessly into our clutches. At home our coloured and Bushman nurses would send us to sleep with stories of animals, birds, streams and trees, which were part of the response of the great Bushman's creative imagination to the reality of his great mother earth.

Laurens van der Post,
The Lost World of the Kalahari

We call nature urihi – our land, our forest. It is the old sky that fell to earth at the beginning. We know that it is alive, that it has a very long breath of life, much longer than ours. With maxitari – the breath of the spirit of the earth – the forest becomes beautiful, rain falls on it, and there is always wind. It breathes, though you don't notice it.

Davi Kopenawa, Yanomami, Brazil

This is our land. Do only people live here?
No, there are also monkeys, even bears.
And where would the monkeys go if we didn't
ask for land for them as well? That is the
way our land is. The land is for everyone,
men, animals and plants. The land is full
of the spirits of our forefathers, it is a
reciprocal relationship. The land is for
our men of today and for our children.
—
Asháninka, Peru

Ownership of the land? We know we don't own it, but we know we belong to it.

Malani Pai, Pai Ohana, Solomon Islands

I lived in the heart of the Borneo rainforest for fifteen months at the tail end of the 1970s, leading a scientific expedition for the Royal Geographical Society in Mulu, Sarawak's newest and largest National Park. Scientifically, the attraction lay in the rich biodiversity found within Mulu's boundaries; the mission of our international team of geologists, zoologists and botanists was to prepare a management plan at the invitation of the Sarawak Government. I also had one fervent hope – that I would meet the Penan people, who depend for almost all their needs on the bounty of one of the most ancient forests on earth.

About 12,000 Penan live in the state of Sarawak, mostly in the watersheds of the Baram and the Rejang rivers, although today only a few hundred still lead a largely nomadic way of life. They know every inch of the territory through which they move, following the migrations of wild bearded pig that they hunt with hardwood blowpipes, the darts tipped with the poisonous sap of the ipoh tree. Their staple diet is the starchy pith of the wild sago palm: only one or two trunks are harvested at a time, leaving the palm to resprout so that there will always be fresh food the next time their carefully planned migrations bring them back to the same place. In the normal course of events, when there is no logging, supplies of both sago and wild pigs renew themselves plentifully during the months before they are gathered or hunted again.

The nomadic Penan seldom stay in one place for more than ten days at a time; when game and fruit become scarce they move on, trading meat and other forest products – camphor, wild rubber and incense wood – for knives, pans and tarpaulins. Once they have left a camp, there is virtually no trace of their passing, for they live in harmony with their environment and a respectful, sustainable attitude to their natural world is as instinctive as breathing. This gentleness of spirit extends to their societies: their egalitarian culture is dominated by the principle of sharing, and the greatest crime is to be selfish. Stay peaceful is their law.

For the first couple of months in Mulu we met no Penan, although we found abandoned sulaps, their lean-to shelters, and were told by the Berawan tribe that they were probably watching us from the cover of the forest. Then one day, out of the blue, Nyapun arrived. A muscular Penan headman carrying a blowpipe, he wore a bamboo quiver in his bark loincloth. He walked into the clearing between the river and our longhouse camp and shook my hand; our connection was instant. Early the next morning he took me to meet his family, a full day's fast walk far out in the forest. Neither of his two wives or ten children had seen a European before, but they greeted me calmly, fed me on heart of palm, smoked mouse deer, river prawns and sago sweetened with honey. We bathed in the stream beside their three palm-roofed sulaps and that night they danced in the firelight. Of all my encounters with forest peoples, my meeting with Nyapun's family was undoubtedly the most pure and magical. He was to become my constant companion for those fifteen months and remains one of my dearest friends.

I grew to love the Borneo rainforest, and for that exciting period of my life it was my whole world, a green home of giant ferns and hanging lianas. It was largely through

Nyapun that I also came to understand it, not only as a result of his extensive knowledge of the flora and fauna, but from the Penan origin myths he related. Years ago, so he told me, Mulu was filled with trees so beautiful that they fell in love with each other, and entwined in an arborescent embrace of roots and vines and branches. Humans witnessed this eternal love and copied it; thus were born the first people – the Penan. I spent my days and weeks walking through this embrace, discovering twisting networks of caves and virgin forest ablaze with scarlet rhododendron.

I remember well an afternoon when, cutting a fresh trail into an inaccessible area of forest we thought had not previously been visited by man, we arrived at a shallow river. There, playing unconcernedly in the water, dabbling under stones for shrimps and catching fish with their bare hands, were Anyi, Nyapun's daughter, and her baby sister. They looked as self-assured and tranquil as any children playing in a suburban sandpit. All our combined academic wisdom, our modern equipment and safety rules suddenly seemed absurd and artificial beside such serenity and confidence in their environment. By the end of the expedition the scientists agreed that it was the Penan who were the real rainforest experts.

All Penan people still have a harmonious and sustainable relationship with their forest, which is in marked contrast to the devastation from logging over the last thirty years. Since we were there, 90 percent of the accessible forests of Sarawak have been cut down – a rate of destruction twice that of the Amazon. The land has been deforested in preparation for acacia wood and palm oil plantations. Nothing has stopped the devastation, not even endless blockades by the Penan people, trying to keep the chainsaws and bulldozers off their land.

Today, only a few scattered groups of nomadic Penan still live in the damaged, scrubby remains of their once pristine rainforest. The animals are dying and the rivers have silted up. When I last saw Nyapun, he told me how he had been imprisoned for trying to stop a road being built through his home. Instead of being treated with the respect they deserve, as we had hoped, he and his family were taken away from their lands and settled in a 'Penan village' near a hotel; they are selling bead bracelets to tourists in order to survive.

But Nyapun's extraordinary knowledge and understanding of the rainforest is intact, and has been passed on to his children. If the forests can be restored, and if Nyapun and his family, and all other Penan families, can have the right to the land returned to them, then they may regain control over their lives. The developed world may survive the problems being created by a shrinking planet, but without the protection of their forests, the Penan will not. The forest of Mulu is their life, their home. As Nyapun said to me, 'Everyone has to have somewhere and now, we have nowhere.'

———
Robin Hanbury-Tenison, UK

The forest
is our
mother.

Penan, Malaysia

The caribou are everything.
The centre of our whole livelihood,
all of our food, our culture,
our dances, our spiritual
connections are with the caribou.

Norma Kassi, Gwich'in, USA

Tsi Yunwiyah. I am a Cherokee. In the language of my people Ani Yunwiyah, or Cherokee as we are called, there is a word for land: Eloheh. This same word also means history, culture, and religion. We cannot separate our place on the earth from our lives on the earth nor from our vision and our meaning as a people. We are taught from childhood that the animals and even the trees and plants that we share a place with are our brothers and sisters.

So, when we speak of land, we are not speaking of property, territory, or even a piece of ground upon which our houses sit and our crops are grown. We are speaking of something truly sacred.

Is there a people anywhere in the world that does not revere its homeland? Is there a human being who does not revere his or her homeland, even if he or she may not return? We say that reverence for ancestral lands, no matter how insignificant in our own daily affairs, or how far from our own homes, is vitally important for the whole of humanity.

———
Cherokee statement, USA

Our roots are deep in the lands where we live. We have a great love for our country, for our birthplace is here. The soil is rich from the bones of thousands of our generations. Each of us was created in these lands and it is our duty to take great care of them because from these lands will spring the future generations of our peoples.

———
Sioux and Navajo Declaration, USA

This here is my life, my soul.
If you take the land away from me,
you take my life...
—
Marcos Veron, Guarani-Kaiowá, Brazil

We were made the same as the sand,
we were born here. This place is my
father's father's father's land.
—
Bushman, Botswana

In the beginning of time, Kaku Serankua created Earth. He made her fertile and took her as his wife. The world was supported by two sets of four golden threads which were interwoven and attached to the four cardinal points. Where the eight golden threads cross, lies the heart of the world. This is our home, the Sierra Nevada, which is marked out by the 'black line' which defines its boundary and separates it from the low plains which surround it.

The snow peaks and sacred lakes were placed in the middle of the mountains; this, the highest area, is chundua. A mamo [priest] was put on every peak to be vigilant and caring. Every peak has a mamo, just as every house has someone living there. The peaks are like our temples or churches.

When Kaku Serankua distributed the land, he kept the Sierra as a sacred place where wisdom would reside, so that one day it could be taught again to humanity. This is where Kaku Serankua lives now, watching over his creation.

When he came to create the living beings, he gave laws to the four kinds of people – the white, yellow, red and black. Their colours are the same as the four mantles of the earth: bunnekän, the white earth; minekän, the yellow earth; gunnekän, the red earth; and zeinekän, the black earth.

Our breathing is the same breath which springs from the world: the air, the winds, and the breeze. All the races of people are equal; to each was given their own rights and their own laws so that they did not violate their brothers and sisters. Each one of us has been given a path whereby we can come close to God and recognise and know him.

We were shown how to respect all of this. We did not create this law ourselves: it was given to us by Kaku Serankua, our father. He also taught us how to cultivate the land, how to share our goods equally, how to care for the forests, for the different species of animals, for the waters, for the hills; how to care for the sun, the stars, the moon, for the dry and wet seasons; how to cure sickness and treat illness. He gave us knowledge of earthquakes and of everything which comes to pass in the world. All of this was to benefit all of humanity everywhere: in every part of the Earth.

———

Arhuaco creation myth, Colombia

The earth is our
foundation, the
source of our
spirituality, the
fountain from which
our cultures and
languages flourish.
The earth is the
keeper of events
and the bones of
our forefathers,
the substantial
evidence of our
people's existence
before memory.
The earth is our
historian, our
educator, the
provider of food,
medicine, clothing
and protection.

Hayden Burgess, Hawaii

By Dreaming we mean the belief that long ago, creatures started human society, they made all natural things and put them in a special place. These Dreaming creatures were connected to special places and special roads or tracks or paths. In many places the great creatures changed themselves into sites where their spirits stayed. Aboriginals have a special connection with everything that is natural. Aboriginals see themselves as part of nature.

Aborigine, Australia

We believe that all things, plants, animals, people, water, trees, air, rocks and mother earth need to be considered not just in the present, but also for seven generations to come. We are here, after all, because of the foresight of our fathers, and we must be mindful of those yet unborn.

—

Mike Koostachin, Cree, Canada

The environment
is not separate
from ourselves;
we are inside it
and it is inside
us; we make it
and it makes us.

Davi Kopenawa,
Yanomami, Brazil

I stood on a mountainside tracing the grey-green
lines of dwarf willow that marked the rivulets all
around and watching the shadows of clouds drifting
across the velvet bogs. Reindeer herders could
stand like this for hours and sometimes said that
the beauty of the land was the great love of their
life. It seemed almost unbearable that they should
have so few days to drink in the loveliness of each
site. Forests of spindly larches flowed up the
hillsides like splashes, still green in the shelter
of the deeper valleys but already yellowing where
they had thinned out and faded away towards bare
ridges of lichen-speckled boulders.

Piers Vitebsky, *The Reindeer People*

Survival

In times of drought, when the waterholes of the great Kalahari sand-face turn to dust, Bushmen of Southern Africa store water underground in empty ostrich eggs sealed with beeswax, and quench their thirst with the juice of the *tsamma* melon.

From the agriculturalists of the Amazon to the hunter-gatherers of Africa, from the cultivators of the rugged hills of Bangladesh to the hunting peoples of Canada, tribal peoples have found ingenious ways of catering for their needs over thousands of years without destroying their environments.

Sophisticated hunting, tracking, husbandry and navigation techniques have been the creative responses to the challenges of varied, and often hostile, habitats. The survival of the Moken 'sea gypsies' in the Andaman Sea has depended on their aquatic skills in hunting with harpoons for ray, turtle and crab. The existence of the Innu in Canada's sub-arctic has rested on their understanding of the seasonal migrations of caribou across *nutshimit*, their tundra home.

Nature has been closely observed – in the frozen north, in the heart of the rainforest and under the African sun. Such observations have taught people how to hunt wild game and gather roots and berries, how to sense changes in climate, predict movements of ice sheets, the return of migrating geese and the flowering seasons of fruit trees. The Wichí of Argentina catch fish by detecting minute ripples on the surface of rivers; the Hadza of Tanzania listen out for the call of the honey-bird that will lead them to bees' nests in the boughs of baobab trees. The 'Pygmy' peoples of the Central African rainforests mimic duikers to attract them out of the undergrowth for hunting. 'You learn what the land tells you,' says Gana Bushman, Roy Sesana.

Such continuous immersion in nature over thousands of years has resulted not only in a profound attunement to the subtle cues of nature, but in an encyclopaedic knowledge of native animals, plants and herbs; as such their experiences and skills are extremely relevant to the world today. In the Amazon, the Yanomami use around 500 species of plants on a daily basis for food, building materials, hunting poisons – their arrows are often tipped with the poison *yãkoana* from the virola tree – and medicines. Their pharmacopoeia is vital for their nutrition and health – the juice of the cat's claw vine is drunk to relieve diarrhoea, the bark of the copal tree can treat eye infections. Over time, they have developed complex, holistic health systems that combine the spiritual healing of shamans with herbal remedies. As Amilton Lopes Kaiowá of Brazil says, 'We have our painkillers and antibiotics here in the forest.'

Food is invariably seen as a gift from the Earth, not to be taken for granted, so humility is essential. 'We forget, and consider ourselves superior,' wrote an Onondaga man, Oren Lyons. The delicate balance of man and nature has only been maintained for millennia through a respect for its limits. Prudence, responsibility and reciprocity are therefore vital requirements. Hunters ask before taking the life of an animal, and leave grateful offerings to the animals they have killed.

When living on their own lands, employing the techniques and values they have honed over generations, tribal peoples are typically healthy, self-sufficient and happy. 'The Udege soul is the soul of a hunter,' says Pavel Suliandziga from Siberia. 'His soul is alive when he is surrounded by nature.'

In those days my mother always took me with her into the forest to look for crabs, fish with timbó, or gather wild fruits. I would also go with her to the fields when we needed to harvest cassava, bananas, or to cut firewood. Sometimes the hunters would also call me at daybreak when they left for the forest. I went with them and when they killed small game they would give them to me. That was how I grew up in the forest.

Davi Kopenawa, Yanomami, Brazil

A story is like the wind, it comes floating from a far-off place. We are San Bushmen, the sons and daughters of the first people. I, Nqate, live in the Kalahari. I know all the waterholes and pans round here, all the places where the animals come. When it is the rainy time, the animals come close again and fruits grow. If it rained more often, this Kalahari would always hold plenty of food. But sometimes a year will pass with no rain at all.

I am a hunter. I hunt with my friends, Xlhoase the bow hunter, and Karoha the runner, who will even risk death in the most difficult of all hunts, the hunt by running. We know tracking. This is what we are born to do. We talk silently with our hands. And we read the animals' stories.

Today we must be off hunting. That is what we do, that is who we are. Our names have come on the wind to you, but you don't know our stories. My name, Nqate, means 'always walking', Karoha – 'always running'.

We are always looking, always checking for signs, showing each other tracks. Like here, a pair of porcupine has been feeding recently. We walk for hours along the footpath of tracks. To make no sound, we use the language of hands to show each other the tracks – to say how fresh they are – how fast they are moving – the size of the animal – is it male or female? – how strongly is it moving? – will it be the one?

Tracking is like dancing because your body is happy; it is telling you that the hunting will be good. Only on a very hot day can we hunt by running. We try to chase the animal to its death. We can run down eland, we can run down kudu, we can run down gemsbok. Even if we see a springbok, we go after that one. Many times the animal is too fast and we must leave it. That one wasn't meant for us to take, but sometimes our God, Bihisabolo, says, 'I will set one aside for you.' And we wait to feel in our bodies when we will be lucky.

Once we were always near animals. Now we must walk far to find them. We see where a cheetah passed. We put on the cheetah's mind. He is hunting. If we follow him, he will lead us to his kill.

A jackal passed here. The fat tail of a female scorpion shows us the trail is old. For we know the scorpion moves by midnight and her trail lies over the front paw mark of the jackal.

When you track an animal you must become the animal. You feel a tingling in your armpits when the animal is close. Then you know the hunt will be good. You learn the ways of birds that come on the wind. They whisper to you the rain is coming. These are the things we know. Tracking is like dancing. This is the great dance.

Then the springbok heart beats in your ribs. You see through its eyes. You feel its stripe, dark on your cheek. Tracking is like dancing, because your body is happy. It tells you hunting will be good. You feel it in the dance. When you do this you are talking with God.

———

Nqate, Bushman, Botswana

I grew up a hunter. All our boys and men were hunters.
Hunting is going and talking to the animals. You don't steal.
You go and ask. You set a trap or go with bow and spear.
It can take days. You track the antelope. He knows you are
there, he knows he has to give you his strength.
But he runs and you have to run. As you run, you become
like him. It can last hours and exhaust you both. You talk to
him and look into his eyes. And then he knows he must give
you his strength so your children can live.

Roy Sesana, Gana Bushman, Botswana

Eh! Listen ancestors,
we Moken are going out
to sea to harpoon the fish.
Do what you can to make
it possible for us to be
successful with our
harpooning. Our harpoons
must not stray off their
course but go straight to
the head or the tail of the
fish. May our harpoons
hit them! Eh! This is how
those who live on boats pray.
These prayers which are
made to the ancestors are
requests. They are born,
then they die and when
we invoke them like this,
we are successful. We speak.

—— Moken folktale

We work differently. We work
with our arms using machetes.
We use food from the earth,
bananas, pawpaw, manioc,
sweet potato, pupunha and
other fruits like açai, buriti
and nuts – all that's there.
We don't eat like you, there is
no oil or pepper.
The food is natural and we can't
destroy the taste. We eat how
we want. We can't use a lot of
salt because it destroys our
health. Yanomami women get
up early and make the food,
then they go to the gardens to
collect manioc to make manioc
bread. Men hunt. The children
play and learn as nature
teaches us.

Davi Kopenawa, Yanomami, Brazil

My land is very important.
I look for wild roots, wild
fruits and wild animals.
I am used to these for
surviving. I know all the
techniques to survive in this
area because I was taught by
my great grandfathers. My
father took me into the bush
and taught me to survive.

Xawa Gaima, Gana Bushman, Botswana

When I first arrived at what is now known as Gombe National Park in Tanzania in 1960 to begin my study of chimpanzees, I could climb the hills of the rift escarpment and gaze out over chimpanzee habitat that stretched far to the north and south along Lake Tanganyika – part of the western arm of the Great Rift Valley – and inland, as far as the eye could see. From the Peak, a rocky outcrop high on a bare ridge that separated two forested valleys, I could watch the chimpanzees from afar, and began to learn more about their complex society. With the passing years, I became increasingly in tune with the rhythms of Gombe and intensely aware of the endless cycles of life and death in the forest, and the interconnectedness of all that lived and grew within it.

At the time, apart from a few villages and the town of Kigoma, the forest and woodland stretched almost unbroken to the southwest border of Tanzania and beyond. Gradually, the human population around Gombe grew, swelled by refugees from troubled Burundi in the north and over the lake from the east. By the mid-1980s, almost all the trees outside the park had been felled. The chimpanzees were virtually imprisoned in an island of forest surrounded by overused farmland, and the people were struggling to survive.

It is the same throughout the forested regions of Central and West Africa. When the habitat becomes degraded through human exploitation, it is not only the animals – including the chimpanzees – who suffer, but also the people who live there. As human populations grow, trees are cleared for grazing livestock, planting commercial crops and building houses, so the rainforest is increasingly threatened. Even when responsible companies practice so-called 'sustainable' logging, taking out only the larger trees, they open up previously inaccessible forests with roads.

This has allowed the development of the 'bushmeat trade' – the commercial hunting of wild animals for food – as hunters can now gain access along these roads. Unlike the 'Pygmies', who shoot only enough animals for their immediate needs, the hunters from outside shoot everything from elephants and gorillas to rodents and birds. Tons of bushmeat are brought out of the forests at a rate that is absolutely unsustainable. As the animals vanish and as the loggers move on, the Pygmies' home is left barren and silent, their way of life destroyed, their future at risk.

Pygmy peoples are often evicted from the forests without compensation or prospect of alternative livelihood. Sometimes governments view them as 'primitive' peoples who should settle to a life of agriculture. But they are not suited to such a life. Indeed, some have said, 'The forest is our home. When we leave the forest, or when the forest dies, we shall die. We are the people of the forest.'

The fate of the Pygmy peoples, and that of the chimpanzees and other forest animals, is linked to the degree to which we can protect their rainforest homes and control the bushmeat trade. By creating awareness of the plight facing the Pygmy peoples and their ancient forest culture, we can foster a new determination to put things right. Let us hope it will not be too late.

Jane Goodall, UK

There are indeed many Inuktitut words or terms for different forms and conditions of snow. These include snow that is falling, fine snow in good weather, freshly fallen snow, soft snow that makes walking difficult, soft snowbank, hard and crystalline snow, snow that has thawed and refrozen, snow that has been rained on, powdery snow, windblown snow, fine snow with which the wind has covered an object, hard snow that yields to the weight of footsteps, snow that is being melted to make drinking water, wet snow that is falling, snow that is drifting and snow that is right for snowhouse building. Also, Inuktitut has a number of verbs that have snow as their root, including picking up snow on one's clothes, working snow with an implement of any kind, and putting snow in a hot drink to cool it down.

These varieties of snow and ice are things that Inuit differentiate and talk about. People must choose sledge routes, select places where they can make a house, and consider which surfaces are safe to walk or sledge across, decide where to stand beside a breathing hole without making sounds that will reach the sensitive hearing of seals. They also must predict the weather, then accommodate to its vagaries. The language for snow is integral to making decisions that will determine the success or failure of hunting, and has vital importance in assessing the probable degree of comfort and discomfort, as well as the dangers, of even a short journey. There is nothing surprising about the richness of Inuktitut when it comes to snow.

Hugh Brody, *The Other Side of Eden*

The depth of silence was beyond anything I had
ever known, made all the sharper by the occasional
snorting and scrunching of our reindeer on a
darkened slope nearby, each one named, trained,
and bound to us by a loyalty that was ancient,
but could easily be lost.

———

Piers Vitebsky, *The Reindeer People*

There's the stinging bee that nests in trees and another that is found underground, which doesn't sting. There is a little bird called the 'guiding bird'. The people have observed the behaviour of the bird, and can read its signals. If the bees' nest is far, the little bird will disappear for a minute or so before coming back again. If it stays close to the person, it means a bees' nest is near. It then goes straight to the tree and sits on the top without making any sounds. If the little bird starts performing its guiding rituals in places where there are no trees, only bushes and undergrowth, it is probably indicating the presence of a snake, lion, or buffalo, something other than a bees' nest. People know if there are no big trees around where there is likely to be honey, the bird is warning them to be careful. This little bird is known in English as the honey guide. It is so much respected by the people, who treat it like a son or daughter. They know that if they find this little bird they have found food.

Kotsi Mmaba, Bushman, Botswana

We have lived in Mau Forest, on the edge of the Rift Valley in Kenya, for hundreds of years. The forest is an ecological haven and we are conservationists, so we treat it well and live in balance with it. But the climate is harsh and over time we have had to create food reservoirs stored in what we call a 'kesungusiek', a container made from cedar wood and shaped like a beehive.

Kesungusiek were essential; every family had to own one in order to survive the hard times. Children were also taught survival tactics; how to identify edible roots, tubers, wild fruits and herbs for medicines. We harvested honey twice a year based on the pollination habits of the bees and on the trees that flowered during the long and short rains.

We also hunted animals and preserved the meat through drying and smoking. This was the work of men, and it was a measure of their capability to provide stability for the family, and a necessary qualification in being eligible to marry another man's daughter. A man had to show how many beehives he owned and that he was brave enough to hunt even the fiercest animal like a buffalo.

Kiplangat Cheruyot, Ogiek, Kenya

Like all the swineherds in the kurelu, Tukum conducts his pigs
each morning to a predetermined pasture, usually a sweet
potato field gone fallow. Here the pigs eat greens and the stray
vegetables which have escaped the harvest, and root for grubs
and mice and frogs and the small skins along old ditches.
In the afternoon he escorts them back to the village pens,
where they are fed hiperi skins and other offal from the fires.
Each pig is marked almost from birth for a debt – but until the
day of its demise it leads an orderly and pleasant life, prized
and honoured on all sides.

Peter Matthiessen, *Under the Mountain Wall*

We can't make cloth –
in this we are ignorant.
We can't make knives.
We don't know
machines. But our
father's ways –
we know these things.
The rituals for pigs,
how a house is built,
the ways to hunt game.
We won't give them up.

Yali, West Papua

Fine horses and fierce eagles
are the wings of the Kazakhs.
—
Kazakh proverb

The golden eagle was six years old and one of the
berkutchy's most prized birds. I asked him about
the rudiments of training, a naive question for
the secrets of the profession are closely guarded.
He did, however, tell me the basics.

The berkutchy first spends weeks among the
remote eyries of the Jungar, Altai or Tien Shan
mountain ranges, where he risks his life to steal
an eaglet from its nest. From then on a close
relationship is established. The eagle ruler sleeps
beside the eaglet for nights on end and feeds it by
hand for a month. 'And they have a big appetite!'
The eaglet is hooded early on to make it totally
dependent on the berkutchy and the absolute
trust which will last a lifetime is slowly built up.
When the bird has bonded, the eagle ruler begins
to train it to fly from his arm and return. The first
kill cements the relationship. The bird is given all
the meat so it understands that man and eagle are
partners in hunting and are not in competition.
Time and boundless patience complete the process.
—
Christopher Robbins, *In Search of Kazakhstan*

Since we were born we have always lived with the animals.
We were born with the animals and we grew up with them.
—
Molatwe Mokalake, Gana Bushman, Botswana

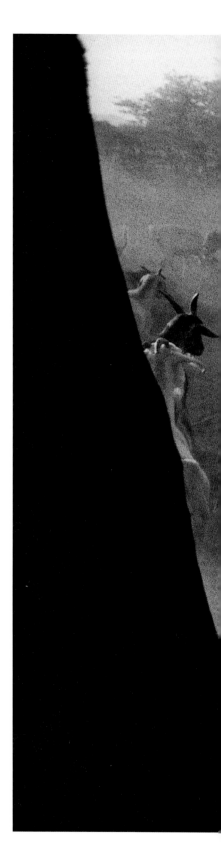

Belonging

On the vast steppe of Mongolia, the doors of the nomads' *gers* always face south, to provide shelter from the icy winds that sweep over the grasslands from Siberia. It is impolite to knock; a visitor must simply walk in. The door may be physically closed, but figuratively it is open: a symbol of the Mongolian nomads' tolerance and hospitality, and a metaphor for their community spirit.

Dependent on each other for survival in remote and often harsh environments, tribal peoples have lived – and many still live today – in complex communities where the solidarity of the group is of utmost importance. Values and social mechanisms have therefore evolved that place the collective over the individual, and emphasise mutual support and sharing. 'We have to work collectively because that is our power and advantage to do so,' says Tanien Ashini, a Sheshatshiu man from Canada. It could be argued that many tribal people have not experienced the loneliness and isolation that have crept into some fragmented western societies.

Kindness and reciprocity are generally highly valued. The Penan's measure of a person's success in life is the strength of his human relationships; the worst social offence is *sihun*, a failure to share. Yanomami groups believe that a hunter will become ill if he eats his own game; others will not carry their own meat back to the settlement, so ensuring the prey is equitably divided. In the North American Indian tradition of *potlach*, status and prestige stems from the number of accumulated goods that are destroyed or redistributed by their owners.

This concept of collective identity also typically extends to land rights – the Penan do not believe in the idea of private land ownership; the Bushmen reject the notion of private property. The ancestral lands of the Maasai of East Africa, are not, as the Maasai politician Moringe Parkipuny says, 'for individual appropriation.' Land is held collectively by most tribal peoples, and communities have a joint responsibility to safeguard it; under many laws, it cannot be bought or sold and a proprietary attitude to the Earth is anathema. 'I don't say that I discovered this land because my eyes fell on it,' says Davi Kopenawa Yanomami, 'it was always there, before my time.' Their homes – the vast palm-thatched structures of the Yanomami that house up to 400 people, the tree houses of the Papuan Korowai, the floating *kabang* of the Moken sea-gypsies – bind the community and anchor them to their territories.

Thus, to say 'we' is far more instinctive than 'I'. Many tribal societies have little formal leadership; decisions are made by consensus and commands articulated only as suggestions. The Bushmen and Yanomami tribespeople, for example, have no official leaders and recognise no 'chiefs'. Of the tribal communities that have not been divided by eviction or resettlement, many consider themselves part of a dynamic, coherent whole: meaning lies in maintaining this sense of belonging as well as kinship with all forms of life. As a continuation of their ancestors, many tribal peoples are also deeply aware of their place in society, and of the unborn generations: the past and future are always contained in the present. 'Men must be born and reborn to belong,' is a Native American saying. 'Their bodies must be formed of the dust of their forefathers' bones.'

The great difference between the indigenous and the Western world is that we live in communities, we feel at home with our brothers of our group, of our people, of our indigenous nation. Together we are strong. The individual is important as a member of the whole. Our ancestors had no experience of Western individualism. We cannot conceive of it for our children.

Evaristo Nugkuag Ikanan, Aguaruna, Peru

With the coming of darkness, families gathered around their hearths to prepare for sleep. As I lay comfortably in my hammock that first night, I felt myself in a kind of fairyland. A tree-rat called and was answered intermittently by one near the river. Six cries followed by seven in a regular series. Owls hooted in the distance, and nightjars whistled loudly to one another with a melodic but monotonous three-tone call that swooped rapidly up the scale and then down again. Frogs and toads croaked and warbled in chorus. Always, in the background, insects chirping high in the trees filled the tropical darkness with a bell-like tinkle.

There was no moon; the only light came from the fires burning in each of the 20 hearths more or less evenly spaced around the perimeter of the yano, and from the faint glow of stars in the sky. When the flames burnt low, I had the sense of being in a vast, underground cave, silent and insulated from the world around. But every now and then a fire would flare up, as one of the women left her hammock to fan the embers. Then the curved roof of the yano was suddenly illuminated, and the sky in the centre became darker by contrast, so that it seemed like a great dome attached to the roof.

Later that night, it started to rain. I could hear the drops pattering on the thatch above my head and could see them falling in the open space in front of me, but no water found its way through the roofing. Sleepless but snug under the watertight covering of thatch, I felt a deep contentment spreading over me. For hundreds of miles in all directions, the forest surrounded me, immense, frightening and utterly different from the world I had just left. But the walls of the yano kept all the strangeness of that vast wilderness at bay. Inside, I felt sheltered not merely by the palisade of leaves around me but also by the companionship of all the other people dozing in their hammocks around the yano. It was as though the whole vast building contained a single family, of which I was, if not a member, at least a welcome guest. I was already beginning to understand.

Robin Hanbury-Tenison, UK

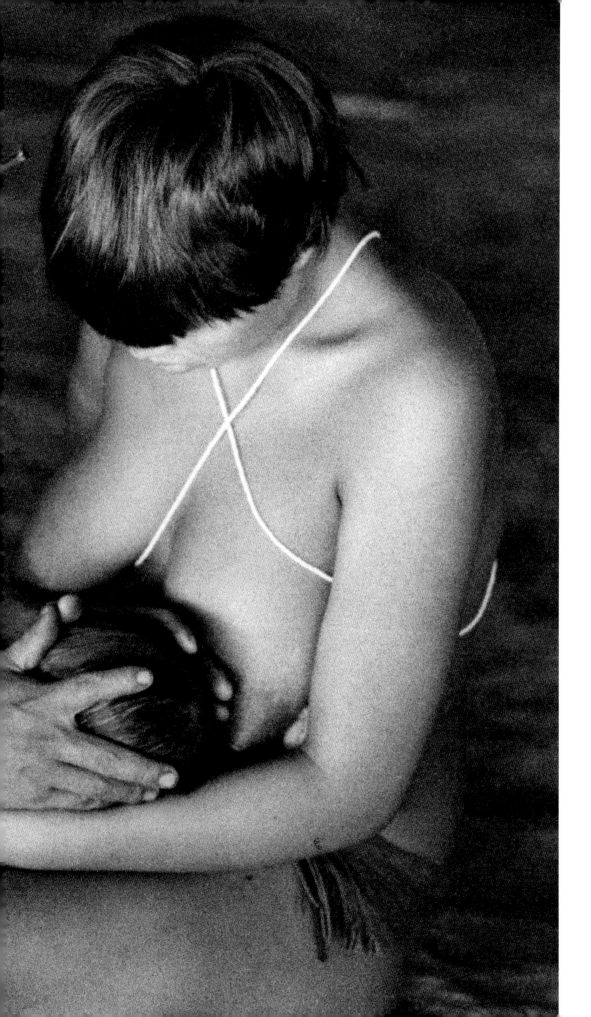

I do not think the measure
of a civilisation is how tall
its buildings of concrete are,
but rather how well its
people have learned to relate
to their environment and
fellow man.
—
Sun Bear, Chippewa, USA

This land is the house we have always lived in.

—

Linda Hogan, Chicksaw, USA

Daily life in Bushmanland revolves around noresi. Bushmanland is our large nore. It is like a territory for all our families. The large nore consist of our small nore which are territories of an extended family. Nore means basically the place where you were born and your parents and grandparents were born. In Eastern Bushmanland, we have 200 of such 'family noresi'. The nore is not just a piece of land. It is a piece of nature. It is our natural resource. We find our entire livelihood in such nore: the vegetables, the wild food plants, the water, the game and material for our houses, tools and so on. Each nore does not provide the same natural resources, therefore, the Juhoan families have learned to share them. We have learnt to help each other in order to survive in such a harsh environment. In short, the nore is our backbone for survival, and therefore the foundation for our culture.

—

Kxao Moses, Juhoan Bushman, Namibia

The icy breeze burnt our faces and froze our breath, weighing down the delicate strands of our wolf-fur hoods with frosted beads, turning our nostril hairs into icy needles. I cried out with excitement as we shot over the ice and immediately felt the lining of my lungs freeze.

My Inuit friends and I clutched on to one another as we careered over the sea-ice. Beneath the hard cobalt-blue sky, my team of huskies fanned out on their traces, tails held proud and purple-pink tongues lolling.

There is nothing quite like shooting across the sea-ice on a dog-sledge – knowing that the ice beneath the creaking sledge is the only thing between you and thousands of metres of hypothermia-inducing Arctic waters. It is out there in the polar wilderness that one gets a unique perspective on life.

Suddenly, Piuartoq cracked his sealskin whip over his huskies and urged them to stop. The dogs held back, whimpering at the smell of the sea. Ahead was an open lead of water, gleaming darkly like a fresh wound in the ice. Piuartoq turned to us, concern etched in his face. In just a few hours, he said, the whole ice pan could break up.

Until recently, the Inuit hunters of the Thule district in north-west Greenland have relied on the ice to reach the remote areas where they can find game. Now with the effects of global warming, the ice is unstable. Sometimes it doesn't appear at all. Without the ice, the Inuit are confused. They have lived with it for centuries; without ice they are lost.

I was 10 months old when my father – pioneer and polar explorer Sir Wally Herbert – first took my mother, Marie, and me to live in the Arctic. My father's affinity with the polar regions stemmed from 14 years of mapping the wilderness of both the Antarctic and the Arctic, and from his British Trans-Arctic Expedition. His skills for such an epic journey were learnt during his many long journeys with the Inuit (or Inughuit) of the Thule district. It seemed the most natural thing in the world to take his young family to live with these strong people, for whom he had developed a great respect and admiration. Our destination was Herbert Island, a small sliver of land off the extreme north-west coast of Greenland – home to one of the last surviving hunting villages of the Inughuit. The ways of these hunters were those of their ancestors. Clothing was still made from furs; the men wore sealskin kamiks [boots] with polar-bear trousers and tugto [reindeer] parkas; the women wore kamiks and fox-fur pants. The men still hunted with harpoon in skin kayaks in the summer, and drove dog teams for hundreds of miles across the sea ice in the inky darkness of the four-month-long winter. While they were away the women would sew furs and skins for clothing, tend to the children, and cure or cook seal meat, whale and fish.

By the time we left Herbert Island – over two years later – I spoke only the local dialect of Greenlandic and believed that I was a little Inughuit girl. Finally, after many years of absence from my childhood home I concluded that something was missing from my life. I had to go home to the Arctic.

I expected much to have changed, but I was unprepared for the extent of those changes. Herbert Island is now deserted. The settlements seem little more than an annexe of Scandinavia, with tourist-class hotels and brightly painted wooden homes nestling between snakes of steel service pipes supplying electricity to the prefab houses. The environment seems essentially the same – the tundra is still covered with purple saxifrage, green mosses and Arctic poppies with blooms the size of a newborn's fingernail; Arctic hare, snow bunting, seal and narwhal still proliferate. Look a little closer, however, and one discovers the unhappy effect of climate change and pollution. For centuries the Inughuit have survived on a marine diet rich in iron, protein, omega-3 fatty acids and essential vitamins – one that until now has prevented heart disease and ensured that the people can withstand the rigours of such an extreme climate. Yet this same diet that has given them life, and defined their culture, now threatens them.

The Arctic has become a dumping ground for the world's toxins. Currents drive industrial chemicals to the Far North, where they are unable to break down and enter the polar ecosystem. Recent studies have found that the fish and animals that the Inughuit hunt carry some of the highest levels of toxic compounds on earth, and as a result, the Inughuit also have dangerous levels of highly toxic pollutants in their bodies. Inughuit women have been advised to stop breastfeeding as the level of chemicals in their milk is toxic.

'They tell us that we must not eat mattak [whale blubber],' my friend Tekummeq tells me, 'but this is all we know. Eating Inughuit food makes us who we are!' She swings her arm towards the ice. 'And now the ice is changing, too.'

Since the 1970s conditions have indeed changed dramatically. The temperatures in Greenland have risen by more than 2°F (1.1°C) – twice the global average – the vast ice sheet is melting at an alarming rate, and the sea ice in some places barely freezes at all. The people are becoming increasingly disorientated because their way of life is constantly in a state of flux. Hunters are cautious when travelling. The ice, they say, is not as truthful as it once was. 'When you were a child,' an old hunter friend of my father told me, 'the ice was strong and faithful; now it tricks us, many fall through it. Some do not come home from hunting.'

A hunter's senses are his most infallible guide in an environment where the weather is notorious for its unpredictability: blizzards and thick fog often obscure landmarks. The scent of the air, for example, can advise him of conditions and how close he is to land, while his super-developed eyesight can distinguish what type of ice lies in the distance by looking at the patterns in the sky. The bend of the ice beneath his feet will usually tell him its depth, age and density; he can taste snow on the air and even hear the vibration of the land itself.

However, changes in currents and temperatures mean that solid-looking ice may have been invisibly corroded.

'I think we are very strong people, because the weather is so strong,' Tekummeq says. 'But now your weather is coming to us. Soon maybe we will have no ice. If we have no ice, we will have no dogs. Who will we be then?'

———
Kari Herbert, UK

In the Verkhoyansk Mountains of
northeast Siberia, Eveny nomads are on
the move. Teams of reindeer pull
caravans of sledges down the steep slide
of a frozen mountain river. Bells tinkle
on the lead reindeer while dogs on short
leashes dive closely alongside through
the snow like dolphins beside a boat.
One man sits on the lead sledge of each
caravan, his right foot stretched out in
front of him and his left foot resting on
the runner ready to fend off hidden rocks
and snagging roots. Passengers or cargo
sit on the sledges behind. The passage
of each caravan is visible from afar by a
cloud of frozen reindeer breath.

This is the coldest inhabited place on
earth, with winter temperatures falling
to -96°F (-71°C). The ice is a condition
of the water for eight months of the year
and by January it is six feet thick.
Throughout the winter, warm springs
continue to break through the surface of
rivers, where they erupt as frozen
turquoise upwellings, like igneous
intrusions in rock, and freeze into jagged
obstructions. Caravan after caravan jolts
over the last ridge of river ice and skims
across a great frozen lake in an epic
sweep stretching almost from shore to
shore. Deep lakes provide a more level
surface and the ice that forms from their
still water glows black, marbled with
milky white veins snaking into the
depths. The sudden speed and the spray
of ice crystals flung into our faces
behind the hypnotic flash of the
reindeers' skidding hooves make it easy
to feel that we are about to take off and
fly into the air.

Piers Vitebsky, *The Reindeer People*

'**After a night of partying with the whole village, dancing and singing around a fire,** six or seven of us, men and boys, arranged to go on a walk through the forest to see one of the rope creeper bridges over a river. We set off across a track past some huts and into the bush, balancing along thin slippery logs. The path was very narrow, often unrecognisable, with very low branches. We blundered along tripping, slipping and crashing around; the 'Pygmies' with their dainty bare feet were silent.

We were in primary forest with tall, tall trees, dense vegetation and leaf litter beneath us. All was quiet except for the Pygmies' singing and chatting to each other. They communicated when apart by banging the buttress roots of the trees with big sticks, producing a sound like very loud drums, as well as making hollow sounding claps.

Now and again our friends pointed and stared at the tops of the trees above us but I could never see or hear anything. Only one of them carried a bow and arrow but never used them. Twice they spotted bees' nests in the top of vast trees and one of the younger blokes zoomed up a hundred feet in a few minutes – incredible, straight up the creepers, like some small Tarzan, big muscles and wide, alert eyes. I'd never seen anyone climb a tree so fast before – fantastic – and straight down the vine even faster.

Whilst walking, some of the men would take a short cut from behind us then run at full speed on either side of the path through the dense forest as though it was an open field – unbelievable. Meanwhile, we were still stumbling along the path at a rapid walking pace. We passed through an old village of seven beehive shaped huts in a ring – each a framework of interwoven twigs covered in a layer of vast leaves. Eventually after two hours of solid jungle we arrived at the Epulu River, a very wide brown water river with dense forested banks. We crossed the river in a dug out canoe poled by one bloke; very unstable, almost rolled over. On the other side we found that it was 'the end of the road' – there was no bridge. They obviously thought we just wanted to see a river! Good all the same, we hung about, the Pygmies caught a load of fish, don't know how or where from, they just went off and reappeared with fish wrapped in leaves a few minutes later. We walked back the same way even more rapidly. Very tiring following these small powerful men, each only up to my chest in height. Arrived back, tired, sweaty and thirsty and sat with all the villagers and recovered. All seemed pleased at our safe return!'

I wrote these diary notes whilst walking, hitchhiking and painting for a year in 1983/4 across Africa; it depicts part of a day spent with the Pygmies in what was then Zaire. The experience illustrates Pygmy peoples' hospitality and genuine kindness together with the satisfaction and contentedness in their own lives. At the time it all seemed so complete and sustainable. It was only much later, when back in the UK, that we read about the Pygmies' complete lack of representation in decisions concerning their own futures; issues relating to land ownership, deforestation, water access and poisoning. It was only then that we learned about the discrimination and exploitation they face, and how they are ostracised from the whole political process of their country.

Kurt Jackson, UK

As is self evident to the Yaka Pygmies, humanity is a part of nature,
not something that is possible to isolate from nature.

Jerome Lewis, UK

This is a good life.

—

Dawat Lupung, Penan, Malaysia

I was greeted in silence when I visited the Penan. Their gentle, unassuming faces peered down at me in the night from their open-sided shelters. The occasional hand stretched out to greet mine, each remaining soft and unclenched as I awkwardly shook it.

During the weeks that followed I made some great friends in the Malaysian jungle, but we were filming illegally and our programme was difficult to make. It was the last episode of *Tribe* and the one that affected me most deeply.

In visiting fifteen different tribal groups around the world I had long since learnt the dangers of drawing conclusions about any one culture from fleeting visits. Most of our information came from vociferous reading of anthropological texts. By comparison, our programmes were snapshots, but valid nonetheless.

I found the Penan to be the most gracious hosts. They had an unstructured way of life, few rules and institutions. Although I was desperate to avoid over-romanticising their culture, I felt as if they had as close to an egalitarian, anarchic, gender-equal, peace-loving culture as I had ever come across. Despite the absence of rigid rules and institutions, they seemed to have an innate sense of morality.

During my time with them, my friends also showed me one of the last remnants of the primary rainforest that once covered their homelands. It was rich in fruit trees, cool, open forest – noticeably different to the dense scrub of the secondary forest where the animals are dying and the rivers have silted up.

They asked me how I could help to protect these last untouched areas, how I could help to protect the Penan peoples. It broke my heart that I had no immediate answers for them. But I promised I would tell the world their story.

Bruce Parry, Ibiza, Spain

One of the essentials of a good community – that is, a community in which each of us can build flourishing lives for ourselves and those we care about, is tolerance. Tolerance matters for the obvious reason that the diversity of interests and desires people have is sometimes so great that we don't even understand why others should think and behave as they do; and yet we acknowledge their right to do so, because we cherish the same right for ourselves.

It is easy to fool ourselves about tolerance. We think we are tolerant when really it is a case of our not minding what other people choose to be or do. But when we do mind – when we disagree, when we cannot understand or sympathise with the choices others make, and find ourselves inconvenienced by them – then the hard work of genuine tolerance is demanded of us.

The very possibility of society's existence turns on tolerance. There cannot be society, community, family, human groupings, unless people get along peacefully and co-operatively most of the time. We have to recognise the entitlement of others to their choices and give them space accordingly; we require no less for ourselves and our own chance of flourishing.

—

A.C. Grayling, UK

In traditional Aboriginal society, no one person was more important than another – all were parts of a whole. Growth and stature were measured by contribution, participation and accountability.

—

Pat Dodson, Aborigine, Australia

Think not forever of yourselves, O Chiefs,
Nor of your own generation
Think of continuing generations of our families,
    think of our grandchildren
And those yet unborn,
Whose faces are coming from
    beneath the ground.
—
Peacemaker, Iroquois Confederacy, USA

The Moken are born, live and die on their boats, and
the umbilical cords of their children plunge into the sea.

Moken oral history

Celebration

In the narrow valleys of the Hindu Kush in Pakistan, the Kalash people celebrate the winter solstice with the festival of *choimus*. In village centres, girls wearing costumes decorated with cowrie shells, and necklaces made from apricot kernels, dance around bonfires singing hymns to the spirit of *Balomain* and offering seasonal foods to their ancestors.

Spirituality runs throughout every aspect of tribal peoples' lives. One widely held belief is that spirits are an integral part of the land; they live in rocks and waterfalls, mountains, plants and animals. Revering the spirits through rituals is a pragmatic approach to the challenges of survival for, in ensuring their ongoing benevolence, the needs of the community are secured.

Dance is one vibrant, ritualistic expression of tribal peoples' spiritual beliefs. The eagle dance of the Hopi people of Arizona worships the relationship between man and eagle; the Dinka of Sudan honour their cattle in their dances; Bushmen of Southern Africa celebrate the ostrich and eland. The most intense dance of Bushmen is the fire dance; to rhythmic clapping and singing, dancers circle the fire, the moth cocoons tied to their ankles rattling with every step. The euphoria induced by the dance can generate *num*, a boiling energy.

Tribal rituals are also linked to the changing seasons and the fertility of nature; they are used to purify the Earth, set the sun on its seasonal course, ensure the fertility of crops and bring success to a hunt. In Brazil, the Enawene Nawe's *yãkwa* festival welcomes the return of men and boys from long fishing trips. In Arizona, the Hopi people sing for rain and for the melting snow to irrigate their crops, while their *powamuy* ceremony marks the first sight of the new moon.

Deep in the rainforests of Central Africa, the 'Pygmy' peoples' haunting sessions of polyphonic singing, accompanied by papaya-branch flutes and harps made from raffia leaves, invoke the *makoondi* – forest spirits – in the hope of securing a profitable hunt.

Festivals also honour the different cycles of human life. The Hopi's *wuwtsim* initiation ceremony celebrates the transition of young men into one of four secret societies, while in East Africa, the Maasai's traditional *e unoto* ceremony heralds the transition of the teenage *moran* into manhood. As well as marking the passage of time, such rites hold communities together, as does their storytelling.

The oral traditions of many indigenous peoples are rich in tales, creation myths and memories that recall mystical creatures and mythical heroes, shape-shifting animals and epic journeys. The Innu storytellers relate how the world was created by wolverine after a great flood; the Hopi that a disc of buckskin thrown in the sky became the moon. Respect for the natural world permeates the stories, which not only help to educate their children about the history of their people, but impart concepts of responsibility and balance.

The exhilarating horse races of the Mongolian nomads, the ancient rock art of the Australian Aborigines and the hypnotic drum dancing of the Inuit evocatively represent tribal peoples' imaginative ways of celebrating life. Some rituals can seem cruel to western thinking; most are now being replaced from within, and cruelty is, of course, found everywhere. With the rampaging force of global monoculture eroding cultural diversity, the variety of tribal rituals is a reminder that human beings have different priorities, and can choose other ways of living.

If you have the heart to feel and the eyes
to see, you discover that the world is not
flat, the world remains a rich tapestry,
it remains a rich topography of the spirit.
These myriad voices of humanity are not
failed attempts at being you, failed
attempts at being modern, they are
unique facets of the human imagination,
they are unique answers to a fundamental
question: What does it mean to be human
and alive?
———
Wade Davis, USA

There were two horse races for animals of different ages: five-year olds in the morning and seven-year olds in the afternoon. The horses were ridden by children between the ages of six and twelve. The tiny kids wore peaked caps and coloured capes; many had no shoes and plenty rode bareback. The race was one straight twenty-four kilometre dash to the finish in town. The horses had been taught not to stop, no matter what happened, and a steed that has lost its jockey is still in the running – traditionally, it can even win the event. As the racing pack neared town the crowd picked up on the shouts of the young riders and abandoned the other events to run over the finishing line, standing on fences or their own mounts to get a better view of the approaching racers. The winning horse was greeted with wild cheers and then named *Tumay ekh* or 'winner of ten thousand'. Meanwhile, its owner won another horse – no small prize – while the victor itself had a poem recited in its honour. The last animal in the pack was also sung a song – not to humble it, but to encourage it on for next year.

Bruce Parry on Mongolian Naadam Festival, *Tribe*

The best world is in the many worlds the world contains.

Eduardo Galeano, Uruguay

Family and well-wishers from all around descend on a Dongria Kondh bride's village to attend her wedding. The air fills with the dusty smell of turmeric, which young women use to stain their arms and faces a rich yellow. It shows off their tattoos and makes them even more beautiful. With flowers in their long hair, and brightly coloured bands around their necks, men and women spin around in whirling dancing circles until someone misses a step and the ring disintegrates into a giggling crowd.

Inside her family home the bride weeps, a piercing truncated wail. Women bring her gifts, sit and sing to her, and the priestess prepares her for the journey ahead. Near dusk the bride emerges, veiled, with two companions and a trail of women carrying her gifts aloft. Around and around the little white hut that is the house of the gods and then, still weeping, towards the narrow forest path that will lead to the groom's village. The wedding guests follow, dancing, singing and beating their drums through the forest, into the night.

Lindsay Duffield, UK

Painting is very important.
It's the design or symbol, power of the land.
First I learned to paint when I was a young man
From my father, Mawalan,
When he take me through the bush, teaching me
        where to go, where to find, what to hunt
And the special places.
Then I learnt Yolnu writing, my own designs,
Drawing on the rock or on the sand
And then putting in the hatching.
I start on the bark maybe when I was about
        fifteen years of age.
But my father was still holding my hand.
I used to shake my hand, but he was holding it.
And he always said to me, 'Hold your brush
        straight,
Paint away from your body. Use your wrist with
        the brush.
Just put the line there. Most important is the line.
Most important is the animal you draw,' he said
        to me.
He still talks to me today,
How to record
And put the line straight and true.

After two months he let me go by myself,
He was still watching.
I sit with bark on my lap, or on the ground,
And then he's holding my hand, helping me with
        the brush,
Rest a bit so the cross-hatching can dry.

I see the designs on my body
Paint on for a circumcision first, to make me
        young man,
But, before that, I saw some other people who
        painted them
On their bodies when they first come to Yirrkala for
Special ceremonies,
Like Djankawu ceremony…

Wandjuk Marika, Aborigine, Australia

Aboriginal artists say that it is difficult to find any Aboriginal art that is devoid of spiritual meaning. Art is their culture, their work, their worship, their history. A painting is more than a painting. It is a chronicle of their country, a map of myths, a memoir of the great spirit ancestors of the Dreamtime. And their paintings are inextricably woven with their love of the land; they are 'dancing, singing and painting for the land'.

Damien Hirst, UK

As I watched, a young man strode up to the edge of the group carrying the long, loosely spiralling horn of a greater kudu antelope. He put his mouth to a hole in the horn and blew four loud blasts, so deep that I felt them vibrating through my body. Screaming and howling, the dancers scattered, knocking me over. Four or five warriors collapsed and lay on the ground, quivering and groaning. People tried to pull them to their feet, but they seemed to be unconscious. They growled, drooled and vibrated their lips. Their heels drummed on the ground like the last spasms of the dead.

George Monbiot, *No Man's Land*

Our ancestors led our people beyond their farthest horizons. Their strength and might may be seen in our legends as well as in the size of our land. With their gleaming spearpoints and broad shields, they acquired the best grazing land in East Africa, the pride of any herder. They played their parts well, and we are proud of them for it. If this noble race of men must now be humble and destitute because of the passage of time, we do not have to accept disgrace and the disappearance of our race. We must adapt to new situations in order to survive. I do not underestimate the challenges ahead, but we must stand up to them in the way we conquered Endikir Ekerio, our legendary escarpment, and the many famines and wars of the past. Our spearpoints are now like the teeth of infants, and it seems the wisdom of the elders no longer counts, but we must survive. We must not follow the way of those races of men who have vanished from the surface of the earth. We have our culture and our governments behind us and our courage, pride, and noble truth. All we need now is determination, and jointly with all other African peoples we will not only survive but multiply and prosper.

Lemeikoki Ole Ngiyaa
from *Maasai* by Tepilit Ole Saitoti
and Carol Beckwith

The darkness fell quickly because of the rising storm, and the dance of the Eland naturally made way for the greatest of all the Bushman dances: the Fire Dance. Here the women, without a pause, grouped themselves singing in the centre of the clearing. Quickly they piled a fire there, lit it the classical way, and then an uncle of Nxou's led the men in a ring dancing around the fire. They danced the first Bushman soul setting out in the darkness, before mind or matter, to look for substance for fire. They looked in vain for its spoor in the sand as if fire were some subtle animal. Hour after hour they went round and round in the same circle without finding it. They called on the sun, moon, and stars to give them fire... Because it was a sacred dance we noticed how in the progress of his search the seeker now acquired the power of healing. Suddenly he would break off his dancing to stand behind a

moaning woman and, with trembling hands draw out of her the spirit that was causing her unrest, emitting in the process the cry of the animal with which the alien invader was identified...

How the dancers found the power to go ever faster and faster, hour after hour, seemed beyond explanation or belief. They danced so hard and long that the circle in the sand became a groove, then the groove a ditch high up to their calves. Long before the end they seemed to pass over into a dimension of reality far out of reach of my understanding, and to a moment and a place which belonged only technically to the desert in which we were all gathered...

All the while, in the ebb of the music rising and falling like a tide around us, the noise of the thunder rose louder in our ears. The lightning began to play incessantly overhead and to wash the dancers yellow in a Nibelungen gold

It sounded as if the whole of nature was being mobilised to participate in the expression of man's first and still unfulfilled quest. The jackals, hyaenas, the shriek owls, the male ostriches booming, all seemed stirred to howl and scream as never before, and beyond the sipwells the lions roared back deeply and most strangely at them, at us, and at the storm...

At last, here and there, a dancer began to fall in his tracks. The two older women would pick him up and carry him aside where he lay moaning in a trance of fatigue in the darkness. Then, almost on the second of midnight, the hero of the dance, Nxou's slender and comely uncle, suddenly found fire the way it was meant to be found. He knelt down reverently beside it, the singing died away in one last sob of utter exhaustion, the dancers sank to the earth while the man picked up the coals in his naked hands and arose to scatter

them far and wide for all the world to share. He stood there swaying on his feet, the sweat of an unimaginable exertion like silk tight upon his skin, dazed with the anguish of near-disaster in doom of eternal darkness as well as by the climax of deliverance. Swaying, he made a gesture and uttered words of prayer to the night around him. What the words were I never knew, except that Dabe said they were too ancient for him to understand... In the darkness beyond the sipwells, on the high dunes at the back of the heroic dancer, the lightning struck with a savage, kriss-like cut at the trembling earth, so near that the crackle of its fire and the explosion of the thunder sounded simultaneously in my ear. And at that moment the rain fell.

———
Laurens van der Post,
The Lost World of the Kalahari

Different people, different ideas and different beliefs make life so much more interesting.

Cecilia Mitchell, Mohawk, USA

Many years ago, my father, a great storyteller, told us that when it was a good year no one went hungry. Inuit would build a big igloo called a qalgiq-qaggiq and celebrate the passing of winter through drum dancing, throat singing, wrestling and other festive games. But it was huqulaniq – drum dancing – that dominated our activities.

Drum dancing was sacred and spiritual. It was also a form of merriment and entertainment. When there was enough light from the qulliq [seal-fat lamp], drum dancing provided an opportunity for men and women to show off their best rhythms.

Women usually sang the songs – songs of men of long ago. Being extremely good singers, the women would either sing alone or with several other women, to accompany and challenge the drummers. I can and do sing myself, as do other men, but I prefer the accompaniment of women. I never tire of their singing.

I can still see my father drum dancing. He danced with great joy to my mother's singing, chanting loud cries and reaching innermost insights and outer spirits – making a connection to the past and to the land. The land is about stories. Inuit simply means 'the people', those who live here. We are the place.

———

Peter Irniq, Inuit, Canada

Storytelling was a form of communication as well
as entertainment.
It brought the past into the present. It connected
children to their ancestors. It filled the tent with
images that danced in the imagination.

—
Norman Hallendy,
Inuksuit: Silent Messengers of the Arctic

For the Enawene Nawe, life is lived through ritual.
The spirit world is ever present and an integral part
of life. Maintaining balance and harmony with nature
and the spirit world is essential.

The universe has two levels; they live between the two.
The upper level is the home of the 'enore nawe' or celestial
spirits, who are the owners of honey and flying insects.
They accompany the Enawene Nawe on fishing trips and
expeditions to gather forest produce, and protect them
from the dangers of the world beyond the village. The
subterranean level is the abode of the 'yakairiti' or spirits
of the underworld whose favourite dwellings are the rapids
and hills.

One of the Enawene Nawe's most important rituals is
'yãkwa', a four-month exchange of food between humans
and spirits. It begins when the õha plant flowers and men
and boys set off for the fishing camps, a day by boat from
the village. They build intricate wooden dams across the
smaller tributaries of the mighty Juruena river and place
woven baskets along the dam to trap the fish.

From the smallest child to the oldest man, everyone lends
a hand whether diving into the water to retrieve the baskets
full of gleaming fish, or gutting and smoking them in the
smokehouse.

Two months later the men return to the village and food
is ritually exchanged with the spirit world in elaborate
ceremonies. Feather headdresses and special costumes are
worn, and men play flutes while different clans chant old
songs and dance around open fires. The singing starts
before dawn and some dances last for hours.

Fiona Watson, UK

I have built my house on the earth and my
children and grandchildren are happy around me.
I have built our church on the earth and our naked
feet have made the earth hard as we dance.

—

Akawaio, Guyana

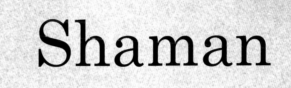

Shaman

From the permanent snows of the Sierra Nevada mountain peaks in Colombia, Arhuaco Indian shamans keep watch over the world.

They call themselves *hermanos mayores* – the older brothers – and believe that they possess a mythical understanding, a profound awareness, of the true nature of existence. Through a system of payments to the Earth, they keep the natural world in balance.

Shamans have traditionally occupied unique positions in many tribal communities. The name, 'shaman', is thought to originate with the Evenk people of Siberia, but shamans have a place in many tribal societies: from the prophetic *Karais* of the Guarani in Brazil, to the rain-making *Emuron* of the Turkana in Kenya and the *Angakkoq* of the Greenlandic Inuit.

They have many roles. Any attempt to define or generalise shamanism would be simplistic, for its mysterious functions are as diverse as they are elaborate. Typically, however, shamans are men and women who specialise in communicating with the natural world and its spirits: people who have a heightened sense of awareness of the divine and the intangible. They are said to possess magical powers, to be able to cross the divide between the human and spirit realms, journeying between dimensions to cajole and appease powerful forces that are invisible to many, yet obvious to a few. This they do both for the benefit of their community and for humanity as a whole.

They are variously healers, priests, custodians of their peoples' sacred rituals, weather diviners, cosmologists, dream-tellers and keepers of botanical knowledge. Guided by spirits and the wisdom of their ancestors, they are called upon by their people to talk to the dead, banish malevolent spirits from the sick, caution the winds and retrieve the lost souls of the unhappy. As healers, they focus on the interconnections between individuals, family and community, and see physical, mental and spiritual elements of health as inseparable.

Through dreams, altered states of consciousness and trances that are aided by hallucinogenic plants, drumming and ecstatic dances, they are believed to transcend the physical limitations of their bodies and the boundaries of human consciousness to travel through time and space. From these worlds between worlds, they study the past to determine the secrets of their peoples' origins.

Inuit shamans talk of flying on journeys through the upper and lower worlds, across the arc of the Milky Way, or diving to the blue depths of the oceans to appease watery spirits. The souls of Siberian shamans can soar across the mountains in search of the animals seen in their visions, while in the Amazon, they can take many shapes; the Tukano, for instance, believe they can transform into jaguars, the most powerful animal in the forest world.

Tragically, colonists, missionaries and governments, wary and contemptuous of shamanic powers and their influence within their tribes, have persecuted them. As there is still much that is not understood about the workings of the Earth and the potential of the human mind, however, it might be wise to pay attention to the insights of those who have a holistic view of life: to people who believe that nature is regulated by subtle powers beyond the reach of science. In the words of anthropologist Claude Lévi-Strauss, 'That the mythology of a shaman does not correspond to an objective reality does not matter.'

When for the first time you sniff the powder produced from the yakoanahi tree, the xapiripë spirits begin to gather around you. First, you hear from afar their chants of happiness, faint as the hum of mosquitoes. Then, when the eyes are dying off, one begins to see scintillating lights trembling up high, coming from every direction in the sky. Gradually the spirits reveal themselves, advancing and retreating with very slow dance steps. They are very small and painted in brilliant colours. Their heads are covered with white hawk down and their armlets are full of macaw and parrot feathers. They dance in a circle, unhurriedly.

—

Davi Kopenawa, Yanomami, Brazil

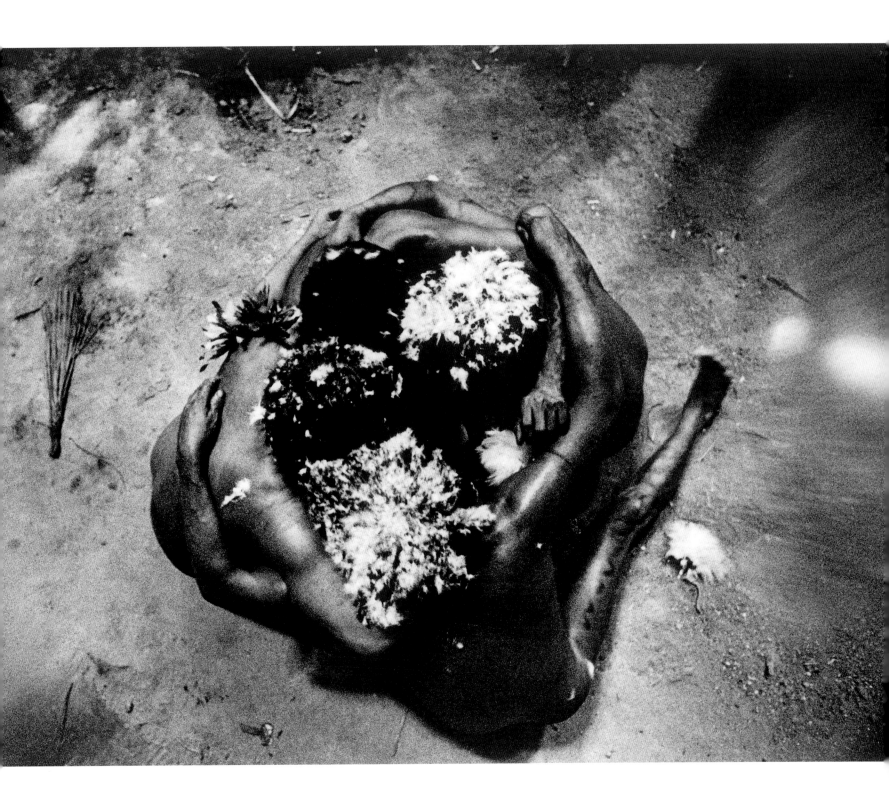

The role of the shaman is that of a leader because he is the person who knows things. He knows the spirit and can divine what will happen today. He knows everything.

—

Amilton Lopes, Guarani-Kaiowá, Brazil

The peaks are like people, like us in many ways, like guardians of honour. They are like our parents, our fathers and mothers.

Arhuaco, Colombia

It is the mamos, our priests, our scientists, who sustain the spirit world. They keep all these forces in balance. They move between chundua, the peaks, and the 'black line' on the plains. They sing and dance, keep the ceremonies, and make payments to the Earth; they keep the sacred objects, the sticks, masks and sacred stones. They are intermediaries who know how to move between the spirit world and the ordinary world. They cure sickness, and can locate the right places for us to bury the dead. They do this not for themselves, not just for us, but for all of humanity and all of life.

These are the true laws which were given to each of the continents. Every creature and every aspect of nature has its own law and, to preserve it, we must respect it. That is how it was ordered, and that is how it always was.

This wisdom, this law, was not invented by us nor by any other person; it is the knowledge which is based on the profoundest awareness and insight. The highest point of all lies beyond the four cardinal points. There, a knowledge resides which tells us of the past, present and future times, of everything which affects the world, the waters, and the different planets. It tells us how to balance the many aspects of nature, so that everything is kept in harmony always. It has been handed down from mamo to mamo, from generation to generation, since the most ancient of times.

Arhuaco philosophy, Colombia

I was all alone on the hilltop. I sat there in the vision pit, a hole dug into the hill, my arms hugging my knees as I watched old man Chest, the medicine man who had brought me there, disappear far down in the valley. He was just a moving black dot among the pines, and soon he was gone altogether.

Now I was all by myself, left alone on the hilltop for four days and nights without food or water until he came back for me... I was sixteen then, still had my boy's name and, let me tell you, I was scared. I was shivering and not only from the cold. The nearest human being was many miles away, and four days and nights is a long, long time. Of course, when it was all over, I would no longer be a boy, but a man. I would have had my vision. I would be given a man's name. Sioux men are not afraid to endure hunger, thirst and loneliness, and I was only ninety-six hours away from being a man.

For us Indians there is just the pipe, the earth we sit on and the open sky. The spirit is everywhere. Sometimes it shows itself through an animal, a bird or some trees and hills. Sometimes it speaks from the Badlands, a stone, or even from the water. That smoke from the peace pipe, it goes straight up to the spirit world.

I wanted to become a medicine man, a yuwipi, a healer carrying on the ancient ways of the Sioux nation. But you cannot learn to be a medicine man like a white man going to medicine school. An old holy man can teach you about herbs and the right ways to perform a ceremony where everything must be in its proper place, where every move, every word has its own, special meaning. These things you can learn – like spelling, like training a horse. But by themselves these things mean nothing. Without the vision and the power this learning will do no good. It would not make me a medicine man.

Darkness had fallen upon the hill. I knew that hanhepi-wi had risen, the night sun, which is what we call the moon. Huddled in my narrow cave, I did not see it. Blackness was wrapped around me like a velvet cloth. It seemed to cut me off from the outside world, even from my own body. It made me listen to the voices within me. I thought of my forefathers who had crouched on this hill before me, because the medicine men in my family had

chosen this spot for a place of meditation and vision-seeking ever since the day they had crossed the Missouri to hunt for buffalo in the White River country some two hundred years ago. I thought that I could sense their presence right through the earth I was leaning against. I could feel them entering my body, feel them stirring in my mind and heart.

Sounds came to me through the darkness: the cries of the wind, the whisper of the trees, the voices of nature, animal sounds, the hooting of an owl. Suddenly I felt an overwhelming presence. Slowly I perceived that a voice was trying to tell me something. It was a bird cry, but I tell you, I began to understand some of it. A voice said, 'You are sacrificing yourself here to be a medicine man. In time you will be one. You will teach other medicine men. We are the fowl people, the winged ones, the eagles and the owls. We are a nation and you shall be our brother. You will learn about herbs and roots, and you will heal people.'

Lame Deer, from *Shamanic Voices* by Joan Halifax

When I'm dancing in the trance dance I start to talk with the ancestors to help me heal the sick person. I became a healer because once when I was sleeping, I dreamed I was a healer. So it came to me and I started dancing and healing. I was still a young person when I became a healer. I dreamed and the dancing and healing started. When I started to dance the trance dance I could feel a person by their blood and smell, and I would go to that person and start healing them.

When I fall down, I feel the blood of the ancestors and talk with them, then I feel the person who is sick. So when I fall down and sleep in trances it's because I've taken something from the blood of the sick person.

When I'm dancing, I start to feel worried about the sick person and I feel that I'm in the mood for healing. The ancestors speak through my blood. I feel something happening, something spiritual. When I touch the person, I'm looking for where the sickness is in that person. I can see the ancestors with my eyes when I'm talking to them in the trance dance.

Xlarema Phuti, Gana Bushman woman, Botswana

Baltazar laughs, his laughter ringing as always halfway between a guffaw and a cackle. His eyes are almost imperceptibly crossed, as if drawn by the magnetic pull of his fine aquiline nose. His face is deeply ridged and brown but somehow ageless, his hair black and wiry and dishevelled. His grin, wide and irresistible, subsides quickly.

I have known Baltazar for twenty years: in fact, he was the first Matsigenka native I ever met on my first trip to the Peruvian Amazon. But I had never spent much time with him, since I usually only stop off in his village for a few days on my way to more remote settlements in the headwaters. Still, no matter how short my stay, he always comes to visit me soon after my arrival. I often reciprocate by paying him a visit to bring him salt, flashlight batteries, and fresh coca leaves.

He usually insists on starting conversations in broken Spanish, as if to remind me that he still remembers the day when I was just learning to speak the Matsigenka language. He often reflects (with a remarkable, almost photographic memory) on my comings and goings, and reminisces about those who have died since my last visit. Sometimes I tell him about my research: whom I have interviewed, what plants they have taught me about, what insights into folklore, myth, and shamanism I have gleaned. He responds, as always, with his pidgin Spanish, his aloof curiosity, his trademark cackle. But today, as I pay him my habitual visit in the early afternoon, he asks me with an uncommon earnestness to sit beside him on a crisp cane mat. He sits alone and speaks to me in his native tongue.

'Do you remember that story you told me about the shaman whose soul was burned by the missionary's flashlight?'

'Yes…' I hesitated, surprised at the unexpected question. Over the years I had heard about various incidents involving a certain American Protestant missionary who came to the village some forty years before to convert the Matsigenka. The missionary was particularly worried about the villagers' faith in the local shaman: the man was able to cure, the villagers said; he drank the powerful ayahuasca brew and entered a trance; he sang, he shook a magical rattle made from bamboo leaves; he climbed a pole in the centre of the ritual hut and ascended to an elevated platform. Later, they would hear the mysterious sounds of footsteps on the roof thatch, then the sound of wings beating; the shaman, they said, had flown into the heavens, the ayahuasca had transported him to the spirit world. Some time later, they would hear the beating of wings, the rustling of footsteps on the thatch, the crash of the shaman falling back onto the slats of his platform. He would descend from the platform, from the very heavens, singing in an alien voice: he had switched places with his spirit twin. The séance was held in total darkness, lest the slightest glimmer or spark burn the shaman's volatile, soaring soul.

The missionary did not like these pagan goings-on. He was determined to stamp them out. But he was cunning, and, feigning curiosity about the shaman's abilities, he obtained an invitation to observe a séance. He was duly informed about the ceremony's procedures, most importantly the ban on artificial illumination. But the missionary snuck in a flashlight. As usual, the shaman drank the powerful brew, sang his songs, ascended the platform. The mysterious sounds of the shaman's magical flight resounded from above. And in the darkness, someone told the missionary, 'He's gone! He has flown away into the sky.'

Then the missionary flicked the switch and brandished his flashlight like a flaming sword. He climbed up the pole and shone the blinding light down on the prone, groggy shaman.

'An impostor!,' the missionary pronounced, triumphant. 'He has gone nowhere. He is fooling you all. He is a devil-worshipper.'

And so, the story goes, the hapless shaman's soul was burned by the missionary's bright light at the height of his midnight trance. He lost his powers and gave up his shamanic practice for good.

Many weeks before, the incident had been on my mind and I had asked Baltazar whether he was familiar with it.

'Yes, yes, I know that story,' Baltazar had answered. 'In fact that man was my brother. He lost his powers. He left here and returned to his birthplace far away. He died long ago.'

I was surprised. 'Your brother?'

'Yes, my brother,' Baltazar had said, but then he had quickly changed the subject and seemed to lose interest.

But now, weeks later, Baltazar had suddenly brought it up again.

'The shaman who was burned by the missionary's flashlight,' he continued, 'you asked me about him last time you were here. I told you that was my brother.'

'Your brother,' I repeated, 'Yes, your brother.'

'I lied,' he said with an inscrutable smile. 'That was not my brother. That was me.'

I was dumbstruck.

'But whoever told it to you got the story wrong,' he continued. 'They said the shaman lost his soul and never made ayahuasca again. I didn't lose my soul. I still make ayahuasca. I'll make it for you some time.'

A few days later, Baltazar came unexpectedly to my campsite just after dark and announced, 'I have made ayahuasca, like I promised. Come drink ayahuasca with me. I can show you many things. Will you come?'

And so on a balmy moonless night I finally learned the truth about Baltazar: his bamboo rattle, beating like the wings of a bird to stoke the flames of trance; his songs, telling the history of his people and the ancient mysteries they guard; his spirit twin, singing in chorus with his own uncannily doubled voice. The sky itself bowed down before him, descending to earth time and time again at his bidding. His shaman-soul was never burnt or lost, just lying low. Wry, cackling Baltazar: the secret shaman all along.

———

Glenn Shepard, Brazil

One of the keys to ensuring cultural
survival is the existence of sacred places.
For my people, among whom I was born
and grew up, the purpose of sacred sites
is to pay tribute to and honour those
gone to the 'upper' world. I always make
a sacrifice every time I make a fire.
My parents were reindeer herders.
I watched the rituals almost every day,
but I was never given any explanations
for the beliefs; that was taboo. Sacred
sites represent the 'owners', that are the
spirits of the sea, rivers and mountains.
People must relate to the owners as they
would to any other powerful person –
with respect. If a human treats a sacred
rock with respect, he may benefit in
return with success in hunting or a
speedy trip through the area. If a human
offends a sacred site by acting badly,
then evil will result.

———

Alona Yefimenko, Even, Kamchatka, Siberia

At night, silent, sitting outside their houses on their stools, the old men would watch the sky. They tracked the movement of the planets, noted the colour of the stars, judged the depth of the haze around the moon, sought shadows in the air – certain, discreet signs they could explain to me. But there were others they could not describe: the invisible manifestations of Akuj, the god of the sky. Their divination was a matter of survival. Growth and desiccation are so rapid in those savannahs that the Turkana must anticipate the rain: the herders must start moving towards it before it falls. Somehow, working with elemental signs unrecognised by Western meteorologists, with a sensitivity that may be inseparable from spiritual enlightenment, the old men were nearly always right.

George Monbiot, *No Man's Land*

The shaman, a mystical, poetical, and political figure... can be described not only as a specialist in the human soul but also as a generalist whose sacred and social functions can cover an extraordinarily wide range of activities. Shamans are healers, seers and visionaries who have mastered death. They are in communication with the world of gods and spirits. Their bodies can be left behind while they fly to unearthly realms. They are poets and singers. They dance and create works of art. They are not only spiritual leaders but also judges and politicians, the repositories of the knowledge of the culture's history, both sacred and secular. They are familiar with cosmic as well as physical geography; the ways of plants, animals, and the elements are known to them. They are psychologists, entertainers, and food finders. Above all, however, shamans are technicians of the sacred and masters of ecstasy.

—

Joan Halifax, *Shamanic Voices*

The shaman learns to pray: there are different prayers to guard against snake bite, attack by jaguars, for sun and for rain. The shaman lives like a spirit and has in his head a telephone line to God.

—

Guarani-Kaiowá shaman, Brazil

He was the keeper of his people's memory,
of their stories and traditions and of his own
inherited secrets. He had knowledge of
death. He knew the ancestral spirits, and
may even, in trance, have recruited or
repulsed them. Sometimes he gave them
peace. Yet he was separated from his
community, often feared. He was called
upon not for simple healing, but to cure
deeper sickness.

———

Colin Thubron, *In Siberia*

Wisdom

Each tribal society is unique. Many, however, have an ancient trust in the harmony between man and nature and the belief that for nature to endure, a long-term attitude to the caretaking of the earth is fundamental. The Iroquois of North America always consider seven generations ahead in their decision-making – a philosophy echoed by Gana Bushman Roy Sesana, when he says, 'We are not here for ourselves. We are here for our children and the children of our grandchildren.'

Perfect conservationists they may not be, but as many tribal societies still depend today on their local environment for all their needs, they are perhaps more aware of the necessity for ecological balance than those who are removed from the natural elements that sustain life. They see that once the forests, trees, mountains and oceans have been depleted, mutilated or polluted too severely, no technological quick-fixes will restore them. To take more than is needed or to degrade the earth is not only self-defeating, but a neglect of their unborn children.

All tribal wisdom has been amassed orally. 'Australia's true history is never read,' wrote an Aboriginal poet, 'but the black man keeps it in his head.' Of the world's 7,000 languages, 4,000 belong to indigenous peoples, yet linguists believe that a mother tongue is now lost every two weeks. When a language dies, a unique perception of the world disappears, for indigenous languages are centuries-deep in insights concerning families, work, love, living and dying. They are also languages of the land, suffused with vocabularies that contain complex geological, geographical and climatic information that is both rooted in their locale, and universally significant.

This wisdom may not be written down, posted to a blog, or studied in a school; it may be articulated through the media of myths and poetry rather than through scientific terminology, but that makes it no less valid or relevant. 'I cannot read,' says Roy Sesana, 'but I do know how to read the land and animals. All our children could. If they couldn't, they would have died long ago.'

It is ironic that as ecosystems are destroyed, so the cultures with an understanding of them are also threatened. Many areas that are the richest in biodiversity remain so due to the care of the people who live in them; the Jarawa, for instance, inhabit the remaining tracts of virgin rainforest in the Andaman Islands. It surely stands to reason, therefore, that the best way of protecting fragile ecosystems, as well as defending the rights of vulnerable peoples, is to secure the land rights of the indigenous communities.

It does not make sense to disregard the wisdom of those whose long-term approach to and knowledge of the natural world have been informed by experience over millennia, when we do not yet know the full scope of what it is we are losing. With traditionally low-carbon lifestyles, tribal people are well placed to give advice on the solutions needed to mitigate climate change. They believe they can influence the choices that humanity faces. 'Only we, the indigenous people, know how to protect the forest,' says Davi Kopenawa Yanomami, 'give us back our lands before the forest dies.'

A thousand years ago the Iroquois' Peacemaker is said to have gathered warring Native Americans together, and placed in their hands the protection of all life forms. He was asked for how long this responsibility would last. 'That's up to you,' he replied.

We descended on the Yali people at Ilamik out of the blue but were received like long-expected guests: a pig slaughtered and a space made for us on the ground floor of the men's hut.

We'd walked for several arduous days from the Baliem valley, West Papua, over high mountain passes and through dense mossy woods, my aim being to find a village that was still close to the forest and relatively undisturbed by the outside world. There I planned to make as broad a study as possible of the complex relationships between the people and their plants. For the Yali have an extraordinary knowledge of the flora and fauna that surround them, and of how to manage them sustainably.

After a while the villagers came to understand what it was that I was doing, if not precisely why, and to help enthusiastically with my information gathering and specimen collecting. I spent the next weeks tramping through their spectacular forests and valleys in the company of men and boys, the men teaching me and the boys singing and running and firing arrows at luckless birds, while I stumbled and slipped and cursed my way in clumsy boots over treacherously slippery log walkways and precarious vine bridges.

During this time I learned an enormous amount about how the Yali coexist with their natural surroundings and rely upon what the forest has to offer. With patience and humour they taught me about edible fungi, tree-fern leaves and nuts of the forest. Like other forest peoples, the Yali people excel as ecologists, recognising at least 49 varieties of the sweet potato and 13 varieties of bananas.

They taught me how to make fire by friction with no more than a stick and a strip of split rattan and how to weave a string bag from the fine bark fibres of Pipturus, a relative of the stinging nettle. They showed me the frames on which they grow the vines whose elongated gourds are worn as penis sheaths, and the pools in which they plant the sedges for making grass skirts. Certain trees are known to harbour large edible grubs in their trunks when they die, and are therefore regarded as secondary food sources. Piglets are weaned by carrying them around in a string bag lined with Breynia leaves, whilst the aromatic leaves of certain wild gingers are wrapped around sweet potatoes during cooking or fed to dogs to make them better hunters.

One evening an elder of the village shuffled over as I sat by the remnants of a fire, lowered himself onto a banana leaf, and began to teach me, hesitantly and cautiously, about the magic plants of his world.

He showed me plants which ensured the death or ruination of enemies, the fertility of crops, the arrival or absence of rain, the willingness of a girl, the shortening of a journey or the success of a hunting trip. He taught me about plants which could drive ghosts and sickness from the village, rats from the fields and wives and pigs from another man's house. So secret and powerful were the plants, he sometimes only whispered or mouthed their names so as not to speak them aloud.

'But now, of course', said the young man who was translating, 'since the missionaries arrived further down the valley we don't believe any of this any more.' I hope he was wrong. The look on my old teacher's face told me he was.

William Milliken, UK

We are educated in the things we know. We can pass on our knowledge to the rest of the world. I can be a lecturer, even though I have not been to school.

—

Daquoo Xukuri, Gana Bushman, Botswana

There are about 7,000 languages in the world, and 40 percent of them are endangered. Every language and culture shows us something unique about the way that a people has evolved to deal with the world around it. Each people solves linguistic, psychological, social, and cultural problems in different ways. So when a language dies, we lose ways of life, solutions to problems, classifications of plants and animals and folk knowledge of the world. We lose myths, folktales, lullabies, songs, poetry and literature.

A renowned linguist once said that when a single language is lost, it is worse than a bomb dropped on the Louvre, for a language is a museum, a repository of knowledge that cannot be replaced. And this is not knowledge that will ever be available on the internet. The more that we lose in terms of diversity of the world's tribal languages and cultures, the more opportunities to solve problems disappear, the more we lose different perspectives that once gone, we can never recover.

Daniel Everett, USA

There lingers this conceit that while we have been busy inventing the internet or placing men on the moon, other societies have been intellectually idle. Whether a people's mental potential goes into technical wizardry or unravelling the complex threads of memory inherent in a myth is merely a matter of cultural choice.

Wade Davis, USA

The ultimate tragedy is not that archaic societies are disappearing, but rather that vibrant, dynamic, living cultures and languages are being forced out of existence. At risk is a vast archive of knowledge and expertise, a catalogue of the imagination, an oral and written literature composed of the memories of countless elders and healers, warriors, farmers, fishermen, midwives, poets and saints. In short, the artistic, intellectual and spiritual expression of the full complexity and diversity of the human experience.

To place a value on what is being lost is impossible. The ecological and botanical knowledge of traditional peoples, to cite but one example, has obvious importance. Less than one percent of the world's flora has been thoroughly studied by science. Much of the fauna remains unknown. Yet a people such as the Haunóo, forest dwellers from the island of Mindoro in the Philippines, recognise more than 450 animals and distinguish 1,500 plants, 400 more than are recognised by Western botanists working in the same forests. In their gardens grow 430 different cultigens. From the wild, they harvest a thousand species. Their taxonomy is as complex as that of the modern botanist, and the precision with which they observe their natural environment is, if anything, more acute.

Such perspicacity is typical of indigenous peoples. Native memory and observation can also describe the long-term effects of ecological change, geological transformations, even the complex signs of imminent ecosystem collapse. Aborigine legends record that once it was possible to walk to the islands of the Coral Sea, to reach Tasmania by land, facts confirmed by what we now know about sea level fluctuations during the Ice Age. In the high Arctic, I once listened as a monolingual Inuit man lamented the shifts in climate that had caused the weather to become wilder and the sun hotter each year, so that for the first time the Inuit suffered from skin ailments caused, as he put it, by the sky. What he described were the symptoms and consequences of ozone depletion and global warming.

Elsewhere in Canada, in the homeland of the Micmac, trees are named for the sound the prevailing winds make as they blow through the branches in the fall, an hour after sunset during those weeks when the weather comes always from a certain direction. Through time, the names change, as the sounds change as the tree itself grows or decays, taking on different forms. Thus, the nomenclature of a forest over the years becomes a marker of its ecological health and can be read as a measure of environmental trends. A stand of trees that bore one name a century ago may be known today by another, a transformation that may allow ecologists, for example, to measure the impact of acid rain on the hardwood forests. Some botanists suggest that as many as forty thousand species of plants may have medicinal or nutritional properties, a potential that in many instances has already been realised by indigenous healers. When the Chinese denounced Tibetan medicine as feudal superstition, the number of practitioners of this ancient herb-based discipline shrank from many thousands to a mere five hundred. The cost to humanity is obvious.

But how do you evaluate less concrete contributions? What is the worth of family bonds that mitigate poverty and insulate individuals from loneliness? What is the value of diverse intuitions about the cosmos, the realms of the spirit, the meaning and practice of faith? What is the economic measure of a ritual practice that results in the protection of a river or a forest?

Answers to these questions are elusive, impossible to quantify; and as a result, too few recognise the full significance and meaning of what is being lost. Even among those sympathetic to the plight of small indigenous societies, there is a mood of resignation, as if these cultures are fated to slip away, reduced by circumstance to the sidelines of history, removed from the inexorable progression of modern life. Though flawed, such reasoning is perhaps to be expected, for we are all acolytes of our own realities, prisoners of our perceptions, so blindly loyal to the patterns and habits of our lives we forget that, like all human beings, we too are enveloped by the constraints and protection of culture. It is no accident that the names of so many indigenous societies – the Waorani in the forests of the Northwest Amazon, the Inuit of the Arctic, the Yanomami in the serpentine reaches of the upper Orinoco – translate simply as 'the people', the implication being that all other humans by default are non-people, savages and cannibals dwelling at the outskirts of the known world. The word 'barbarian' is derived from the Greek barbaros, meaning 'one who babbles', and in the ancient world, it was applied to anyone who could not speak the language of the Greeks. Similarly, the Aztec considered all those incapable of understanding Nahual to be mute.

Every culture is ethnocentric, fiercely loyal to its own interpretation of reality. Without such fidelity, the human imagination would run wild, and the consequences would be madness and anarchy. But now, equipped with a fresh perspective, inspired in part by this lens brought to us from the far expanses of space, we are empowered to think in new ways, to reach beyond prosaic restraint and thus attain new insight. To dismiss indigenous peoples as trivial, to view their societies as marginal, is to ignore and deny the central revelation of anthropology... Just to know that such cultures exist is to remember that the human imagination is vast, fluid, infinite in its capacity for social and spiritual invention.

Our way of life, with its stunning technological wizardry, its cities dense with intrigue, is but one alternative rooted in a particular intellectual lineage. The Polynesian seafarers who sense the presence of distant atolls in the echo of waves, the Naxi shaman of Yunnan who carve mystical tales into rock, the Juwasi Bushmen who for generations lived in open truce with the lions of the Kalahari, reveal that there are other options, other means of interpreting existence, other ways of being. Every view of the world that fades away, every culture that disappears, diminishes a possibility of life and reduces the human repertoire of adaptive responses to the common problems that confront us all. Knowledge is lost, not only of the natural world but of realms of the spirit, intuitions about the meaning of the cosmos, insights into the very nature of existence.

Wade Davis, USA

My name is Roy Sesana; I am a Gana Bushman from the Kalahari, in what is now called Botswana. In my language, my name is 'Tobee' and our land is 'Tamm'. We have been there longer than any people have been anywhere.

I am a leader. I cannot read, but I do know how to read the land and the animals. All our children could. If they couldn't, they would have all died long ago. I was trained as a healer. You have to read the plants and the sand. You have to dig the roots and become fit. You put some of the root back for tomorrow, so one day your grandchildren can find it and eat. You learn what the land tells you.

I know many who can read words and many, like me, who can only read the land. Both are important. We are not backward or less intelligent: we live in exactly the same up-to-date year as you.

If anyone has read a lot of books and thinks I am primitive because I have not read even one, then he should throw away those books and get one which says we are all brothers and sisters under God and we too have a right to live.

Roy Sesana, Gana Bushman, Botswana

The San Bushmen represent a 100,000 year-old culture that we should consider one of the world's treasures. And while progress is necessary, it cannot be that the only way to achieve progress is to remove the San from their ancestral lands and drive their traditions away.

When a culture is destroyed in the name of progress, it is not progress, it is a loss for our world. Hundreds of thousands of years of wisdom, knowledge of nature, medicines and ways of living together go with them.

Desmond Tutu, South Africa

I have met the happiest man on Earth, Elías Hualinga, 'Cucharita', whose only possessions were his canoe, his bows and his hut. He always had a kind word for his neighbour, his friend or a foreigner; he was always happy, always smiled, even the day I visited him on his bed where he was in great pain due to a wrongly diagnosed malaria. He was still smiling when he said to me, 'My little brother, I am dying now, I am going with my little God.' I shall never live my life again in the same way as before, even in my native Europe.

I have worked in the Amazon for twenty-six years and can say that I have learnt from the Amazon Indians some of the greatest lessons of my life. I come from a culture where the future is almost more important than the present, where so many people live obsessed by the accumulation of things; where so many are fixated on the past and traumatised by the uncertainties of the future; where emotions, personal relations and even friendships are frequently sacrificed for material possessions; where people hide behind masks, titles and social conventions and hardly relate to each other as human beings.

Among other things, which would fill whole books, I have learnt to put my western worries in perspective. I have learnt to see life from a more humane, natural standpoint, to derive more enjoyment from human relationships, family and sincere friendships, from the little moments and little things that add up to make life a gratifying experience instead of one that is pain-strewn.

When I arrived in the Amazon I found it hard to understand how people who had no material belongings, who lived on a knife-edge of survival, who knew that illness could kill them at any point and who did not know whether they would be able to find food for their children in the forest from one day to another, could be so happy. I started to feel guilty for worrying about an uncertain future when I could see beside me people who were happy without the surety of a tomorrow.

To witness the integrity, the humility, the resigned and deeply human sagacity with which many Amazon Indians face adversity and terrible misfortunes without losing their joy of living, their sense of humour and the warmth of their relationships; to see how they face death as naturally as they live life, has helped me to face my own inevitable anxieties in a wholly different way.

The French writer Marguerite Yourcenar used to say that a man belongs not to where he is born, but to where he feels intelligent for the first time. I learnt to live in the Amazon, and so that is where I belong. When I feel worried, I remember an Amazonian saying: 'Tomorrow will also be a day.' When I sense depression, I think of another saying, 'Nobody dies on the eve of his death.' When I get obsessed by how I will cope in old age, without the 'honourable' retirement pension that every Westerner aspires to have, I think of my Amazonian friends, so content despite their many problems. And I feel envious, because their ability to live and enjoy the present is not poisoned by the past nor mortgaged by the future.

José Alonso Álvarez, Peru

We watched from the shore as our canoe floated off into Utshisk-nipi. It was a fine summer's morning, and I was deep in the interior of sub-Arctic Labrador with two Innu hunters, Dominic Pokue and Daniel Ashini. We had been on our way to Seal Lake, to look for caribou. We were 90 miles from the nearest village in an area usually accessible only by plane. Everything we had to survive was on the canoe: food, clothes, tent, sleeping bag, guns, traps, a generator and a satellite phone. I was worried.

I was about to start swimming out to the boat but the water, only free of ice for about three weeks was extremely cold. After stepping in I quickly realised that I should head back. We could only watch as the boat drifted further and further out into the lake. We tried to follow it from shore, following an old Innu trail through willow thickets and spruce forest, scrambling from unyielding rock to soggy marsh and moss. But it was impossible. And even though Dominic would have been able to show us the route home, returning to the village on foot without food, clothing or ammunition was unthinkable. We lit a fire to keep the black fly at bay and alert a plane to our situation, smoked, and thought about our options: we had no food, no shelter and only minimal clothing. Dominic asked me if I was nervous. I told him I was, 'a little'. He replied by saying, 'Don't worry. Even though our things may be lost, we are still alive. Nervousness doesn't help when you are in the country.'

After 36 hours when we had minimal sleep in makeshift beds of spruce boughs, finished the last crust of raisin bread and kept vigil for a plane that never arrived, we had exhausted all our options. So Daniel and Dominic made a small raft by lashing together old tent poles found in a disused campsite and we used it to ford several rivers in search of our lifeline. Finally, we recovered the canoe.

As we sat eating tins of salmon on sunny rocks, I thought of how Daniel and Dominic had saved my life, and how I would have been useless left to myself. Throughout the ordeal humour and warmth prevailed; there was no attempt to blame anyone or assign fault. The canoe was found because Daniel and Dominic had not lost the skills they needed to live in what the Innu call nutshimit – or 'the country'.

But it was not just that they knew how to make a raft and to ford rivers, how to hunt and fish. What helped equally was that they had the mental strength needed to survive on the land in dire circumstances.

The Innu, distinct from the circumpolar Inuit, are the northernmost Algonquin-speaking peoples of North America. They have occupied the area for 7,500 years and their history, skills, cosmology and language give meaning to this landscape of labyrinthine forests, snaking rivers and the tundra beyond. Their understanding of the complex relationships between humans, animals, water and trees is highly developed.

Yet this knowledge, and the way of life on which it is based, has been systematically dismantled. Generations of fur traders started aggressive assimilation policies, which the Newfoundland authorities perpetuated. Missionaries branded the Innu beliefs 'devil worship' and inculcated a psychology of fear in the children. Their land was continually confiscated, with no disguising the desire for natural resources, and the once nomadic people were moved into overcrowded village shacks. The Government mandated that their children should attend schools, so alienating them from their families and criminalised the Innu for hunting caribou, integral to their way of life. In short, they enforced many processes that attempted to alter the Innu and diminish the many sources of their uniqueness as a people – their consensual decision making, their belief in the importance of personal autonomy. By the 1990s petrol sniffing was epidemic and the villages were recording some of the highest suicide rates in the world.

Still, despite the indignity and tragedy of recent years, our experience with the canoe demonstrated that the Innu had not lost the capacity to think as Innu people. In places like Utshisk-nipi, life can be easily compromised by bad judgments, inappropriate temperament and arrogance. Innu believe that lack of humility to the forces of nature can itself be a cause of accidents, sickness and death. Simply acknowledging that one is dependent on nature and cannot overcome it is an act of contrition to the animals, the land, the fish, and all the natural elements that surround human life. This 'respect' is for Innu what guarantees a good life and their identity is in the country. As one Innu man has said, 'My identity, my religion, is in the country. I go to my own school there. There are medicines there that I know about. Out there I am a worker, a fisherman, an environmentalist and a biologist.'

When we appeared to be stranded, we were not stranded; we were simply living in the country. We were living with the exigencies of nature. Nature to the Innu means more than the physical properties of the woods, the waters, animals and the elements; it means an almost ineffable link between people and nature. People are not separate from nature, above it, or in a commandeering position in which all is their dominion. The animals are hunted, it is true, but they are not considered prey. Animal and Innu lives are seen as part of the same order of the world, an order with extraordinarily close attachments between all living things. For hunters, animals do not speak, but they are not 'dumb'. They are as wise as us, and all Innu legends and stories testify to this. The relationship is not adversarial.

When we lost the boat, I was curious to know why such a heavily laden craft moored in sand on a lake with no tides could have so easily come loose. Dominic gave several possible reasons, but would not be drawn on the absolute veracity of any explanation, since in reality, he did not know, and could not have known absolutely why the canoe drifted into Utshisk-nipi. One idea he had, however, was that it was the *katsheimaitsheshu*, spirit figures who inhabit the country. They might have configured themselves into tiny men, and pushed the boat out into the water. 'Why would they do that?' I asked. 'To make sure that we realise that we are dependent on the water, the elements and the animals, and not the other way around. To make sure we remain humble,' said Daniel.

———

Colin Samson, UK

I am the environment.
I was born in the forest,
and I grew up there. I know it well.
Without land and nature,
we can't live, the world can't work.
You talk of the planet, yet you don't
think it has a heart and breathes,
but it does.
You talk politics and study on paper.
But we study in the forest and look
carefully. You don't know our wisdom.
It's very different.
We understand that all living things
have a *noreshi* – another living being
which is born at the exact same time
as yourself.
Your *noreshi* may be a bird, or a boar,
or a deer, or a fish, or an anteater, a
butterfly, or any other kind of living
plant or animal.
It rests when you rest, it feeds
when you feed, it sings when you sing.
It dies when you die.

Davi Kopenawa, Yanomami, Brazil

Today, after so much injustice
and ill treatment, indigenous
people show our destructive and
aggressive civilisation a dignity,
something that we can call,
without any exaggeration, a new
human philosophy.

Jean-Marie Le Clézio, France

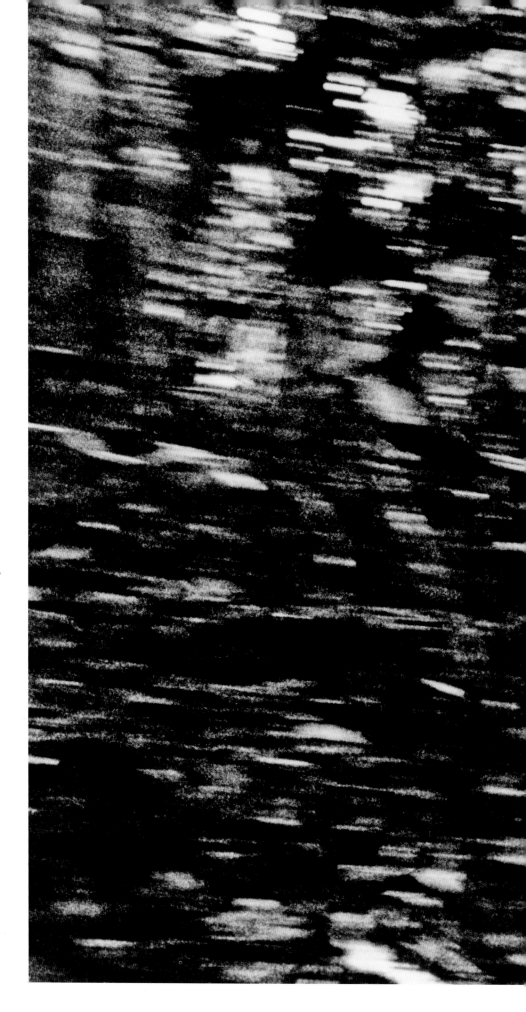

Lying across his hammock, making the most of the final rays of sunlight, Anilton grasped the notebook in which he recorded the events of the Amazonian expedition, and began:

'We walked rather longer than we had planned to find somewhere to spend the night that was not waterlogged. We had to make several stops during the day because Putchá, a 12-year old Awá Guajá Indian boy, had brought some embers with him and needed to stop every so often to attend to the fire that he was carrying. Time and again Putchá would go looking for dry twigs and abacaba leaves to add to the embers. He would then puff out his cheeks and blow, add the sticks and leaves and blow and blow again until he was certain that he had not let the dying ember go out. When this kind of thing happens, all the Indians lie down; a boy comes to suckle at his mother's breasts and another stares upwards; another goes off looking for fruit; another searches for tortoise. And we too have to remove our backpacks; someone takes off his trainers and someone else oils his shotgun. Good God! So much time is wasted. I asked Zé Gomes to persuade Putchá to abandon the embers, as his stops were slowing down our journey. So Putchá went to the foot of a sapucaia tree, dug a hole with his own hands and buried his fire there, still burning.'

After Anilton had noted the day's events, he listened to the Indians talking from their shelters, watched the shadows of the trees dancing in the firelight, and fell asleep.

He woke during the night; the stars had already changed their positions. Anilton saw Zé Gomes get out of his hammock and stagger half asleep to the fire, which was now cold. He saw him squat down, take a charred stick, blow and blow on it until the end went red, bring it up to his face and, drawing deeply, light his cigarette.

'Anilton, are you asleep?' asked Zé Gomes.

'No, Zé. I'm just lying here, thinking about tomorrow.'

'Do you remember Nayá?' he asked. 'The Indian woman we met from the Parakanã group? Do you remember that we went to her hut and she told us that her burning fire – the fire that made her food, burnt her fields, hardened the points of her arrows and lit up the moonless nights – had been passed on to her by her grandmother? And that it had also been her grandmother's grandmother's fire?'

Awakened by Zé Gomes's memory, Anilton felt his head go dizzy and his throat close up, causing a suffocating feeling of anguish. He thought about the fire he had forced Putchá to abandon, and wondered how many loves it had lit, how many childbirths it had witnessed, how many smiles it had illuminated and how many pains it had comforted.

———

Wellington Gomes Figueiredo, Brazil

No new forms of human development and progress can omit tribal wisdom; their memories are worth more than the sum of computers' memories. They have achieved what the modern consuming society has not managed to achieve over the last centuries: a fulfilling, rich life that does not threaten the planet's chances of survival.

All those who are asking themselves what the solutions are to get the world out of the crisis, have the answer in front of their eyes – but are not able to see it. It is necessary for those within the fields of science, research and technology to develop a greater sense of humility, and endeavour to understand the ancient wisdom of indigenous peoples, before it is too late. A curiosity is needed about different ways of thinking and dealing with things: the farmers of the world, the indigenous peoples, the more isolated tribal peoples of the planet.

Carlo Petrini, Italy

The time has come to stop and take stock; the time has come to look at the evidence and ask ourselves where did we go wrong? In spite of the triumphs of science and technology, why do we live in the midst of multiple crises and conflicts? The world view of industrial and technological societies is based in the idea that the value of nature is only in its usefulness to humans. All natural resources are there for human benefit. Whereas the world view of indigenous societies is rooted in conviction that nature has intrinsic value.

All living beings are our kith and kin. We are all related. What we do to nature, we do to ourselves. Human community is an integral part of the earth community. Therefore care of the earth is a primary responsibility of humankind.

Satish Kumar, UK

The path for humanity charted out by capitalism, industrialisation and colonialism has ended in an abyss.

We need another path. And indigenous wisdom provides the road signs for the alternative path.

Indigenous cultures have survived over millennia on the basis of harmony with nature and in society. The practice of harmony is vital for one future. It will not be learnt in business schools and schools of biotechnology. It will be learnt from the school of life.

Vandana Shiva, India

Exile

When the trade winds carried Christopher Columbus to the 'New World' in 1492, it is thought there were between 5–10 million tribal people living in Brazil. Today there are approximately 650,000. When European settlers arrived on the shores of Australia, they declared it 'terra nullius' – land belonging to no one. They overlooked the Aborigines who had lived there for approximately 60,000 years.

The genocide of tribal peoples has been relentless ever since. They have been bombed, poisoned and gunned down by colonisers, armies and racist governments determined to profit from their lands. It is common for at least half of all tribal peoples to die when first contacted by outsiders, as they have no natural immunity to diseases such as measles or influenza that are introduced. Their cultures and spiritual beliefs have been mocked and denounced by missionaries, and by authorities confident in the superiority of western cultures.

Often, the loss and destruction of their lands are at the root of the appalling suffering they face. They are logged, mined, cleared and torched; the people indigenous to them are rarely consulted, frequently evicted and at worst massacred by the invaders who have found their existing tenure of the land an inconvenience. In the name of 'progress', their basic human rights have been entirely trampled on.

Almost all tribes are also vulnerable to enforced education systems that strip away traditional wisdom, to the creation of national wildlife parks that evict them from their homelands, and to assimilation policies that wreck their families. In Brazil, for example, over 40,000 gold-miners invaded Yanomami territory during the 1980s, leading to nearly 20 percent of the Indians dying from illnesses common to outsiders, but unknown to them.

'To join the white man's society' says a Colombian Arhuaco man, 'is to lose everything which is our own.' Resettlement is a bland term for wrenching people away from their lands, homes, myths and memories – in short everything that gives their lives meaning – and imposing on them a 'superior' culture. Relocated indigenous peoples are amongst the poorest in their countries; the trauma of being uprooted annihilates their self-worth. 'First they make us destitute by taking away our way of life', says Jumanda, a Gana Bushman, 'then they say we are nothing because we are destitute.'

Following diamond exploration in the Central Kalahari Game Reserve, Botswana, in the 1980s, the Botswana government expelled the indigenous Bushmen, forcing them to live in camps that have become known as 'places of death', where depression, AIDS and alcoholism are rife. 'If I went to a Minister and said, 'move from your land',' says a Bushman, 'he'd think I was mad.' Yet this is what happened to the oldest inhabitants of southern Africa.

Unemployment, social disintegration, depression, chronic diseases, reduced life expectancy, infant mortality, addictions and suicide are some of the consequences of trying to assimilate forcibly tribal peoples into mainstream cultures. The youngest member of the Brazilian Guarani to commit suicide was only nine years old; in the last one hundred years her people, who were one of the earliest to be contacted after Europeans arrived, have lost almost all their land. Today they are squeezed onto tiny patches of ground surrounded by vast fields of sugar cane. Others camp under tarpaulin by dusty roadsides, as lorries thunder past.

The notion of 'integration' is such a lie. Indians are being invited to give up their material, social, cultural, imaginative, and emotional independence and join in on the margins of a vast society, capitalist and consumerist, that sees no alternative to the immiseration of millions of its people in urban and rural poverty. Take away the Indians' land, their settlement patterns, their hunting areas, their gardens, their kinship network, their dances, their myths, and offer them... television and football, and a miserable shack on the side of a road. What a lie.

Alan Campbell, UK

The Guarani are committing suicide because we have no land. We don't have any space any more. In the old days, we were free. Now we are no longer. So our young people look around them and think there is nothing left and wonder how they can live. They sit down and think, they forget, they lose themselves, and then commit suicide.

Rosalino Oritz, Guarani-Ñandeva, Brazil

From fire and sword to arsenic and bullets – civilisation has sent six million Indians to extinction.

Norman Lewis, UK

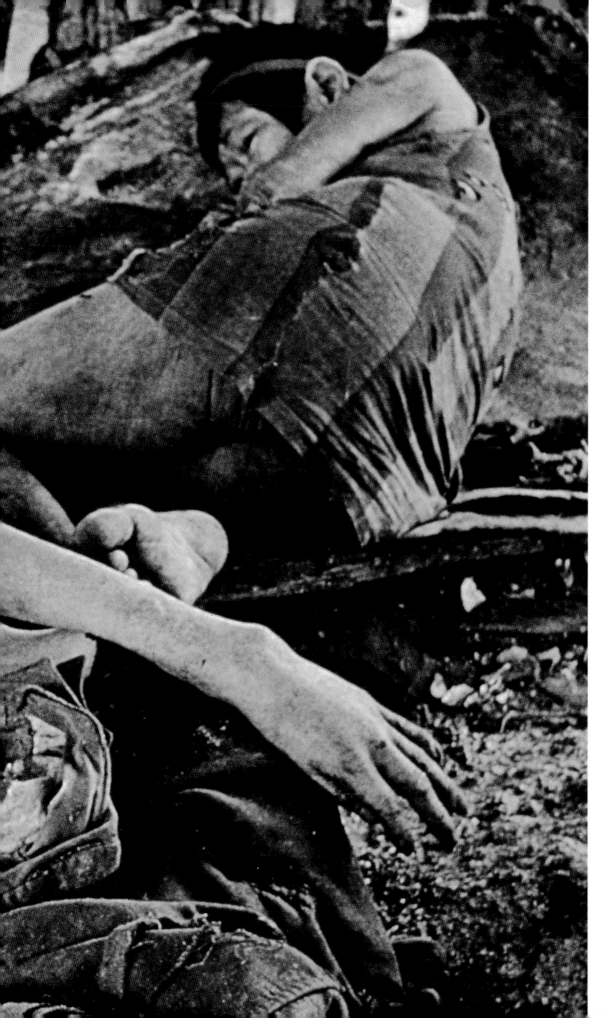

We are plagued with
illnesses these days.
Diarrhoea, malaria
and other diseases like
hepatitis. We didn't have
these diseases before.
We stayed in good health.
We might get a headache,
but we had plant remedies.
But after contact, it has
changed. Now everybody
is constantly sick.

—

Matis, Brazil

169

Why is the government of Botswana persecuting the Bushmen?

Gugama, the creator, made us. That was a long time ago – so long ago that I can't know when it happened. That is the past, but our future comes from the lives of our children, our future is rooted in the hunt, and in the fruits we grow in this place. When we hunt, we are dancing. And when the rain comes it fills us with joy. This is our place, and here everything gives us life. God made us, and He made the animals for us.

Why does the government think they are more important than the people? The government just wants to take all our good things. The government is like a poor fellow who sees a rich man and is jealous and wants to take what he has. Now we must live in the shadow of being thrown off our land. There can no longer be any rest.

I was born in this place and I have been here for a very long time. Now this relocation thing has come, but I don't have the full truth about it. They come and say that I have to move, that this place is for animals. But why must I move and leave the animals? I was born with them and I must stay with them. I have that right.

I was born in this place, with the eland. And we have to stay together. My strength is the force in the animals which my father hunted and my mother cooked. They gave me everything here. This is my birthright: here where my father's body lies in the sand. Who are they who want to chase me from my life which was given to me by God? My father's spirit warned me this would come.

They have already taken my relatives. My brother has been taken and I am here alone. But I am not going to leave. If they want to kill me why don't they just do it? They will kill me for my land.

When they come I say, 'I don't want you to come here, but if you must, then leave your guns behind. If you come with your guns – ready for war – you will have to kill me. I won't do what you want.'

Mogetse Kaboikanyo, Kgalagadi, Botswana

Mogetse Kaboikanyo was a Kgalagadi man who lived alongside the Gana and Gwi Bushmen in the Central Kalahari Reserve. In February 2002 he was forcibly relocated to a camp outside the Reserve. He died four months later. He was probably in his fifties. He was buried in a desolate relocation camp far from his ancestors' graves.

Next to shooting indigenous peoples, the surest way to kill us is to separate us from our part of the Earth.

Hayden Burgess, Hawaii

Those resettlement camps have turned our people into thieves and beggars and drunkards. I do not want this life. First they make us destitute by taking away our land, our hunting and our way of life. Then they say we are nothing because we are destitute.

Jumanda Gakelebone, Gana Bushman, Botswana

Just behind us is an army camp – why? We are encircled.
We are completely at their mercy living here. We are a drowning people.
Life is not ours. I will die but I fear very much for the future of this younger generation
as we don't even know if our existence will continue.

Upendra Lal Chakma, Jumma, Bangladesh

Imagine returning home from school holidays to find your home has disappeared. Imagine discovering that the army has moved in to the place where you have always lived and set up permanent camp. This is what happened to an eight year old Jumma boy in Bangladesh when, after a year away at school, he returned to his village in the Chittagong Hill Tracts to find his parents living in a make-shift dwelling, their belongings scattered. The Government had declared, "We want the land, not the people," and sent in the army to move them out. Hundreds and thousands of Bengali plains' settlers then moved in.

To the Bangladeshi government, the mountainous region of south-east Bangladesh is spare land. Yet the Chittagong Hill Tracts are far from empty. Those in power have overlooked the original inhabitants, for these rugged hills have long been home to the Buddhist Chakmas and other tribes collectively known as the Jumma people. Self-reliant peoples, the Jummas have survived in the dense teak forests for generations, by practising a form of shifting cultivation known as 'jhum'. Gentle, compassionate and religiously tolerant, they differ ethnically and linguistically from the Bengali majority, and are some of the least known indigenous tribes in the world.

Today, they are also one of the most persecuted. Since Bangladesh became independent from Pakistan in 1971, the Jumma people have endured some of the worst human rights violations in Asia. Tribal villages have been razed to the ground. Buddhist monks have been murdered, their temples desecrated. In one single act of genocide, an estimated 1,200 men, women and children were burned alive in their bamboo homes. They have gone from being nearly the sole inhabitants of the Hill Tracts to being brutalised by the military and almost outnumbered by settlers. They have become a minority in their own land, refugees in their own territory – yet news of their persecution has hardly reached the world's press. Despite a peace accord in recent years, the violence and land grabbing has continued and the army still has an intimidating presence.

Sadly, the story of the Jumma peoples is not unique. Time and again, from the Amazon basin to the icy expanses of Siberia, tribal peoples are suffering. Displaced from the lands where they belong, their natural resources are stolen, their ways of life violated, their cultures repressed. Time and again, their voices are not heard.

We cannot pretend this isn't happening, and we cannot let it continue. Ultimately the tragedy of the Chakma and other Jumma peoples – and all the world's tribes – is a sorry reflection on us all. We must speak out against corporations and governments who acquire tribal land and resources without consultation; we must speak out against those who subject tribes to violent repression and abuse. We need to respect tribal cultures – languages, festivals, spirituality, insights into the ways of the world and the workings of the mind – as being just as valuable and precious as any other modern culture. The world's increasingly uncertain environmental future is a reminder that we need to look after our planet and its people, that we are all closely connected and have a responsibility to each other – particularly to those who have no voice.

Richard Gere, USA

Several years ago when
an Innu man went to social
services or the hospital and
was asked his occupation,
he said, 'hunter'. Now, he
says 'unemployed'.

Jean Pierre Ashini, Innu, Canada

For a minute imagine this... You live in a very fine
home, with all the comforts to meet your needs.
But I move into your home, and I start selling off
your furniture and belongings. I receive, say,
$1,000 for the sale and give you one dollar. I tell
you how you should live in your house. I tell you
what you should think about. I tell you how you
should feel and respond to things and when you do
act, I use my values to judge your actions. I tell you
that it is now my house. After a while I suggest that
maybe we could 'negotiate' some changes to this
arrangement, but it will remain my house and I am
in control. The home is of course our homeland,
Nitassinan, and it is Euro-Canadians who have
moved in and taken over. We don't have to imagine
this: we live this experience.

Daniel Ashini, Innu, Canada

175

All the headwaters of the great Xingu river are very polluted. This is because the white people who are agriculturalists throw in toxic pesticides. They chuck everything in there – rubbish, empty cans and bottles of rum. They also kill the wild animals and they leave the dead bodies rotting by the river banks. We Mehinaku use the water to bathe in, to drink from and to fish. We are fisher people – we don't eat red meat. In the Xingu there is a lot of fish, every type of fish. Fish are so important to us and now the fish are dying.
—
Kamalurre Mehinaku, Xingu, Brazil

We, the Penan people of the Tutoh, Limban and Patah Rivers regions, declare: stop destroying the forest or we will be forced to protect it. The forest is our livelihood. We have lived here before any of you outsiders came. We fished in clean rivers and hunted in the jungle. We made our sago meat and ate the fruit of the trees. Our life was not easy but we lived it contentedly. Now the logging companies turn rivers to muddy streams and the jungle into devastation. You took advantage of our trusting nature and cheated us into unfair deals; by your doings you take away our livelihood and threaten our very lives. We want the land we live off, our ancestral land, back. So when you come to us, come as guests with respect. We are a peace-loving people, but when our very lives are in danger, we will fight back. This is our message.

Unga Paran, Penan, Malaysia

The trees hold a very special meaning
and purpose to all living things. They
have provided medicines for our sick and
the materials to build our homes. They
fed our fires so that we could cook our
food and warm our shelters. They shade
us from the sun, shelter the small
animals and birds and most importantly
purify the air that we breathe and the
water we drink. In return they must be
treated with kindness and respect.
Will their kindness to us be forgotten?
Will the respect they are due be ignored?
Will the truth they represent to us be,
quite literally, cut down?

Mike Koostachin, Cree, Canada

We see it like this, it is as if we are all in a
canoe travelling through time. If someone
begins to make a fire in their part of the
canoe, and another begins to pour water
inside the canoe, or another begins to piss
in the canoe, it will affect us all. And it is
the responsibility of each person in the
canoe to ensure that it is not destroyed.
Our planet is like one big canoe travelling
through time. The destruction of the
forest is everyone's concern.

Ailton Krenak, Brazil

The Arctic is not 'wilderness' or a 'frontier'. It is our home and homeland. We Inuit have lived there for millennia. Our culture and economy reflect the land and all that it gives us. Our understanding of who we are comes from the land, and we remain a hunting people of the land, ice and snow.

For decades, Inuit hunters in the Arctic have reported shorter winters, hotter summers, thinner sea ice and accelerating coastal erosion – all as a result of climate change. Hunters have fallen through the sea ice and lost their lives in areas long considered safe. Human-induced climate change is a new assault on the very way of life for us as Inuit. But it is not just a theory to the inhabitants of the Arctic; it is a dangerous reality.

The Arctic is now considered the early warning, the health barometer for the planet. If you wish to see how healthy the planet is, come and take its pulse in the Arctic. Climate change is not just an issue of politics and technology but of human rights. It is also a matter of the survival of humanity as a whole.

Sheila Watt-Cloutier, Inuit, Canada

We are deeply alarmed by the accelerating climate devastation brought about by unsustainable development. We are experiencing profound and disproportionate adverse impacts on our cultures, human and environmental health, human rights, well-being, traditional livelihoods, food systems and food sovereignty, local infrastructure, economic validity and our very survival as indigenous peoples.

Mother Earth is no longer in a period of climate change, but in climate crisis. We therefore insist on an immediate end to the destruction and desecration of the elements of life.

Anchorage Declaration

In India, there's a place where rich forest shrouds the hillsides, where the summer's monsoon rains turn the streams into rivers. India's Niyamgiri hills are home to one of the subcontinent's most vulnerable tribes – the Dongria Kondh. Here, the mountains are revered as gods. In the beginning, their mountain god created Niyamgiri as a homeland for the Dongria. They say he has been watching over them ever since. It's only because the Dongria have known their lands so intimately and for so long, that this extraordinary forest survives.

But now, it is not the bananas or the sweet roots which are attracting outsiders. The mountains are rich in bauxite, the raw material for aluminium; London-based mining company Vedanta Resources is planning a vast open-cast mine on the top of Niyamgiri, the Dongria Kondh's most sacred site.

Vedanta hopes that blasting the top of the mountain away will reveal 70 million tonnes of bauxite. The Dongria know that this will ruin their homes, pollute their lands and destroy their lives.

We cannot let their fate be decided in a corporate boardroom.

Joanna Lumley, UK

Orissa has bauxite mountains, which are beautiful and densely forested, with flat tops, like air fields. They are porous mountains, which are actually water tanks that store water for the fields in the plains. Whole mountains have just been taken away by private corporations, so destroying the forests and displacing the tribal peoples.

Arundhati Roy, India

We believe that there was a mother who had four children. Their mother told them that if the hunger came they should kill her and cut off her head and put it on the top of a mountain. The reason why the Amungme people are working really hard to protect their land is because they believe the mountain area is their mother's head. So now they are gouging out our mother's brains. It's hard to express what has happened to our people. I have only the name, 'Amungme' left. The mountains, the rivers, the forests, all belong to Freeport company and the government now.

Amungme, West Papua

One of the major problems for Indian people is the missionary. It has been said that when they arrived they had only the Book and we had the land; now we have the Book and they have the land.

An old Indian once told me that when the missionaries arrived they fell on their knees and prayed. Then they got up, fell on the Indians and preyed.

———

Vine Deloria Jnr., *Custer Died For Your Sins*

And then someone
obedient and timid settled
down in our souls.
Someone who got accustomed
to being shouted at, someone
who would just humbly beg.

———

Vyachslav Aukhaki, Siberia

For as far as the eye can see there is not a single tree – just an endless carpet of desiccated soya plants withering in the fierce sun. Metallic shards of light pierce the yellow fields. The horizon shimmers in the haze and mini tornados of red dust swirl in the faint breeze.

This is Rondônia state – frontier land, Brazil's wild west, a power house of ranching and agriculture fuelling the country's accelerating economic growth. It is a land of speculation, where fortunes are made and lost, and the rule of law replaced by the barrel of a gun. In the middle of the endless soya fields and cattle ranches, there is a tiny patch of forest, all that remains of what was once thick, lush Amazonian rainforest. And in the middle of this forest are two small straw huts, home to six solitary Indians.

This is the last refuge of the Akuntsu, once a thriving Amazonian tribe, whose final destruction we are witnessing in the 21st century. In a few decades from now, the silent genocide of the Akuntsu will be complete and an entire people with their own language, their own view of the world, their own unique knowledge will have gone. Humanity will be the poorer as yet another piece of our rich diversity disappears forever.

I visited the Akuntsu because I wanted to tell their story – that no matter who the people, nor how small and fragile, they have the right to life and to choose how they wish to live.

The Akuntsu are sitting in the shade of a papaya tree – all six from three generations on one bench. They look dejected and have hacking coughs. Ururu, the old matriarch, had been taken to town for the first time, for medical treatment and came back with a cold. Now it had infected them all. Having been isolated for so long they have little immunity to any western disease.

Nobody will ever know the full horrors of what happened to the Akuntsu. But as the ranchers' bulldozers moved in and flattened their homes, a few escaped the bullets and fled into the last fragments of forest. The massacre only became public when one of the ranchers' gunmen boasted of the killings whilst drinking at the bar of the nearest town.

Today the Akuntsu flinch when they hear chainsaws echoing through their forest, a reminder of the ongoing destruction of the forest around them. Traumatised they try to tell their story, although nobody has mastered enough of their language to understand it fully. Konibu the elder man lists the names of relatives, massacred before his eyes as the ranchers cleared the land of obstacles including the Indians. Pipuk, the other man, shows me the lead shot in his back when gunmen pursued him on horseback, firing at him as he fled.

Before we leave, the last six Akuntsu dance, a slow, halting shuffle. Konibu, a shaman, plays his flute. The notes are long and tremulous. It is a haunting and deeply moving moment, a stark reminder of the banality and cruelty of a much bigger world out there where profit is worth more than the lives of an entire people.

Fiona Watson, UK

Genocide is not only killing off Indians with gunfire. Genocide is also injustice, collaborating with the aim that the Indian and his culture should disappear. We cannot in the name of development have contempt for the Indian, take his lands, massacre him. Absolutely not.

———

Orlando Villas Boas, Brazil

The first gas bomb landed near my feet. Somebody pushed me into a ditch. I heard stampeding from all directions, and rubber bullets. The Urubu, the Xavante, the Pataxó, the Kaingang, the Kaiowá, the Kaxinawá – all of them warriors – were leading a group of about 100 Indians. But the cowardly police closed off the route. The Indians sat on the ground. I saw then what courage is, what dignity is. Many of us ran off. But the Indians could not dishonour their chiefs, they could not embarrass their women nor their young people. They did not want to feel as ashamed as the Brazilian people who, 500 years on, were treating them even worse than at first contact.

The Church asked for forgiveness 500 years after contact; the government hasn't. In fact the government ratified what it had done, and continued to do worse. Nothing hurt me more that day than seeing the Xavante, the Indian warriors, believing that this time, 500 years on, they would be treated as human beings. They believed it, and I confess I did too.
——
Marina Silva, Brazil

The phrase the 'discovery of America' is obviously inaccurate. What they discovered was an America that had been discovered thousands of years before by its inhabitants. Thus what took place was the invasion of America – an invasion by a very alien culture.
——
Noam Chomsky, USA

The land that the whites called Brazil belonged to the Indians. You invaded it and took possession of it.
——
Megaron Txukarramae, Mentuktire Kayapó, Brazil

Resistance

'Will we let ourselves be destroyed in our turn without a struggle?' asked the Shawnee Indian, Tecumseh, in 1810. 'I know you will cry with me, 'never!'' Nearly 200 years later, in 2004, the Ogiek people of Kenya wrote to the exiled Gana and Gwi Bushmen of Botswana, urging resilience and hope. 'Do not let your persecutors make you forget who you are. Be strong! You will see your lands again!'

Tribal peoples are not doomed archaic societies, destined to die out naturally like 'snow before the summer sun,' as Tecumseh added. They are not people who have failed to keep up to date with the fashions of the 'modern' world. Some do seek material prosperity, but many have no wish to adopt the ways of so-called civilised cultures; indeed it is usually only poverty, not an affluent western lifestyle, that is available to them. They have complex, evolving societies; they are people who have made, are continuing to make – *and have the right to make* – different choices about how to live their lives and how to adapt to a changing world. 'Don't hold us back, we want to move forward,' says Dicao Oma, a Bushman woman, 'we have our own talk.'

What does hold them back are racist attitudes that relegate tribal peoples to the role of 'savages'. Or, just as corrosively, attitudes that romanticise them as environmental heroes, living utopian lives of social bliss uncorrupted by the industrialised west. Either way, their humanity is forgotten. Their knowledge of the natural world is undoubtedly extensive, but that does not make them ecological angels; their natural confidence in their communities is generally strong, but that does not preclude social problems. They are, of course, just as human, with all the same emotions and rights. 'We have these philosophies but it is not something to be romanticised,' said the late Hopi Choctaw artist, Dan Lomahaftewa, 'we were given this life way.'

Despite their terrible suffering, the resistance of tribal peoples today is growing; on every continent, they are opposing the many external forces that threaten them. 'We do exist,' wrote Marta Guarani, 'I want to say to the world that we are alive and we want to be respected as a people.' Essentially, they are fighting for control: for the lands that they use and need to be returned to them, for the freedom to determine their own development, for the right to political representation and for their beliefs to be upheld. And they are fighting tooth and nail those who are ripping out the rainforests, mining the mountains and polluting the Arctic. 'We come from the land,' says Mama Yosepha Alomang from Papua, 'we will die for the land.'

They are, however, still vulnerable, not least the uncontacted tribes of the Amazon and Papuan rainforests. The solution lies in the recognition of two basic rights: to land and to self-determination. The recognition of their land rights gives them the peace and space to maintain their traditional lives and also the time to choose how, when or if to interact with their country's mainstream culture.

Tribal peoples' urgent need is for others around the world to *listen* to them, and to join them in their battle to be seen as equals. As an Innu man says, 'If we join our voices into one, it will make us strong.' The whole world would also be stronger for the survival of people whose philosophies tend to place human values above those of economics, and who view balance with nature as a prerequisite for the future of the planet. Tribal perspectives are as modern as they are timeless; their disappearance would be to the detriment of humanity.

Hear me. Not for myself, but for my people.

———

Black Elk, Oglala Sioux, USA

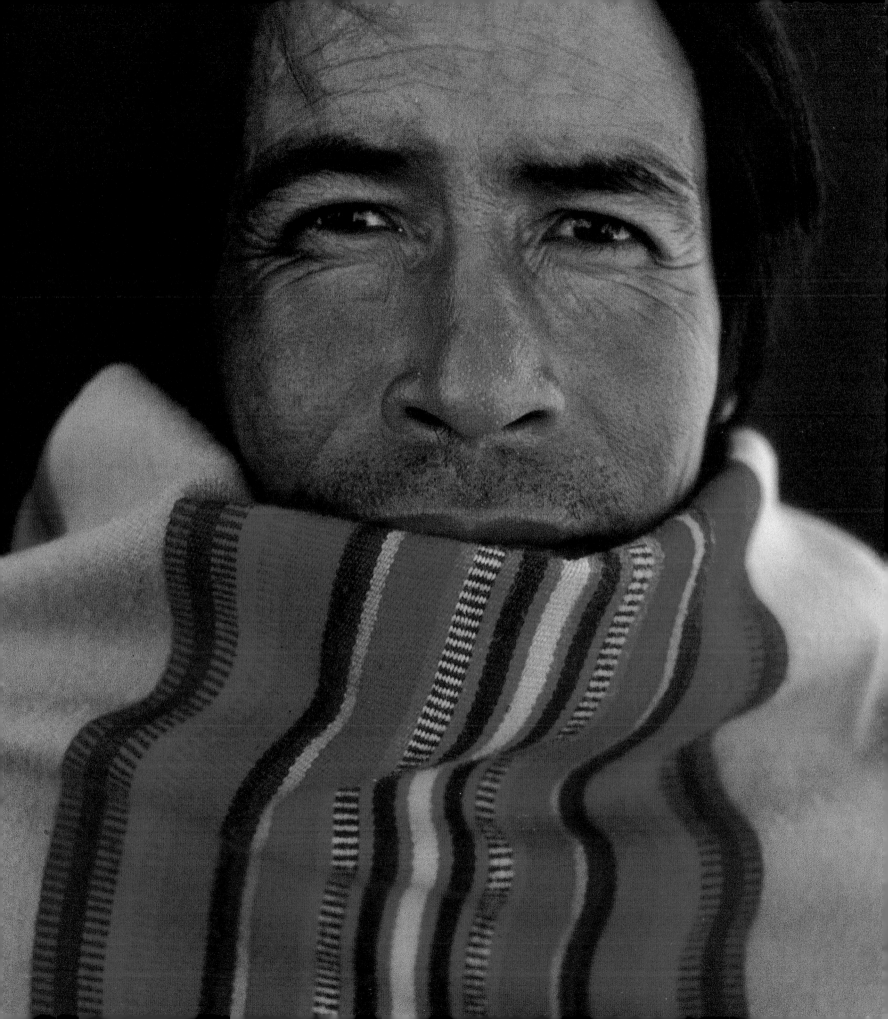

We have the right to be different and free.
—
Guarani-Kaiowá statement, Brazil

It is not that the Yanomami do not want progress, or other things that white people have. They want to be able to choose and not have change thrust upon them, whether they want it or not. I am not saying I am against progress. I think it is very good when whites come to work amongst the Yanomami to teach reading and writing. This for us is progress. What we do not want are the mining companies which destroy the forest, and the miners, who bring diseases, guns, alcohol and prostitution and destroy all nature wherever they go. For us this is not progress. We want progress without destruction.

Davi Kopenawa, Yanomami, Brazil

197

The first step in the
journey and healing
is to reconnect with the
land. It symbolises so
much to us: it is our
family, our parents,
our grandparents.
It is the umbilical cord,
the bond between
mother and child.
—
Doris Pilkington Garimara,
Aborigine, Australia

Aboriginality is not a cluster of behaviours and characteristics that individuals could claim for themselves and recognise in themselves; it is more importantly a characteristic of the continent itself. Australia will be truly self-governing and independent only when it has recognised its inherent and incredible Aboriginality. The island continent was marked and managed by its people for 50,000 years or so. We are only just beginning to recognise how the continuous presence of Aborigines shaped the continent and preserved its fragile eco-systems. It is already too late perhaps for us to learn how to reverse the devastation inflicted by Whitefellas in the short space of 200 years, but some attempt at damage limitation must be made. Recognising the custodianship of the land as a sacred trust would not be a bad place to start.

Germaine Greer, Australia

For hundreds of millennia our species developed in ways that led to relatively modest impacts on the ecological systems that sustained societies. Through insight and learning, leading to folklore and rituals that embodied ecological principles, many human societies adapted their activities and intellectual perspectives to accommodate natural cycles and to manage their exploitation of resources so as to ensure that use was sustained indefinitely. But just a couple of hundred years ago, we embarked on a new direction, bolstered with a new confidence that any problem or hurdle could be overcome with technology.

This view is now deeply ingrained. We have become hooked on an approach that is dangerously over-reliant on one particular form of economic growth. Now confronted with an ecological catastrophe in the form of a mass extinction of species and a pace and scale of climate change unprecedented in human experience, we are finding it extremely difficult to find a different way.

This is one reason why the protection of human cultural and intellectual diversity is so vital. The greatest resource on Earth is not coal, oil or diamonds, but our ability to see things in different ways and to adapt our intellect and culture according to the circumstances that are presented. People have been doing this since humans were human, and that is why we have been so successful.

I have been more and more convinced of the role that the world's indigenous peoples can play in helping humankind. A quick glance at any map which accurately shows recent patterns of deforestation and indigenous reserves across the vast Amazon region makes the point admirably. In many areas outside the indigenous reserves, the process of deforestation is all but complete; where the indigenous reserves have been designated, the forests largely remain. This portrays a very different way of looking at the forests. On the one hand the national energy firms, agricultural commodity companies, loggers and miners see the forests as a source of financial revenue. By contrast, the indigenous communities see in the forests a sustainable livelihood, an irreplaceable heritage that must be passed on intact; they see intrinsic values in the forests that go far beyond its utility and are in tune with the sacred values that they see dwelling in its fabric.

In a world where people's consciousness is controlled by the here and now, it is vital that we find the means to regain a sense of continuity, to reconnect with the past and the future. This is a perspective that is now largely lost to many of us. This perspective of connectedness does remain, however, with many indigenous communities.

Finding the means to inspire new thinking based on different values is surely now one of the most important priorities for western culture. Reconnecting with the world that sustains us is no longer some fringe concern, it is a core necessity for our collective survival.

Through greater respect for the wisdom and cultures of indigenous peoples, the world can not only help to uphold the rights of different groups and to promote justice, we can also find hope for new ways of seeing; go beyond our obsession with technology and progress through growth, to find the means to connect with the planet. In the end, it is the source of all our wealth – spiritual as well as material.

Tony Juniper, UK

I've learned that the fate of the world's indigenous people lies in the fate of us all. And the reason for that is simple. At the heart of today's so-called 'environmental crisis' is something profound and disturbing. We are simply not at one with the world in which we live, we are not 'true dwellers in the land', and behave for the most part as if we were just uncaring itinerants hanging around until we've used everything up and then moving on. For most people in most rich world countries, the visceral connections between people, land, and community have been broken apart.

With that febrile, disconnected, uncaring world now in meltdown, one can only hope that enough people, a little wiser and a little humbler, will understand how much we still have to learn from those who never lost those visceral connections – from the true dwellers of the land.

Jonathon Porritt, UK

We search for your past, your present and future
As your name threatens to disappear from the maps
Changed at the whim of the oppressors...
Don't give up!
Your fighters are the sons of the warriors
Of the ancient Papuan people,
Who are today's warriors?
They may come from any part of West Papua
Papuans from different tribes, with different customs
But one in their determination to win the fight...

Mansoram, West Papua

On the western half of the island of New Guinea, just a few hundred miles north of Australia, a million and a half indigenous West Papuans continue to suffer the consequences of illegal Indonesian occupation. In West Papua you take your life into your hands simply by raising the national flag. Each of the thirteen stripes stands for a West Papuan tribe. The red stripe at the side reminds us of political struggle and bloodshed. The blue and white stripes represent the ocean and the land, whilst the morning star is the star of hope.

It must be difficult to hold onto hope when at least 10 percent of the indigenous Melanesian population has been wiped out by the occupying Indonesian army and when systematic human rights abuses are commonplace. Yet the struggle for self-determination in West Papua, as in other parts of the world, goes on, strongly rooted in hope.

We have a global responsibility to uphold human rights, stand in solidarity with tribal peoples and support the indigenous fight for freedom of expression and independence, if we are to protect our planet's priceless social, cultural and environmental heritage for future generations.

Caroline Lucas, UK

I remember it well; my first encounter with isolated Indians. It was in 1971, our mission was to bring out Jaboti and Makurap tribal people, enslaved by rubber tappers deep in the Amazon. I travelled along the Rio Branco as far as it was navigable, then walked along many trails until the indigenous people accompanying me suddenly refused to continue. They had found signs of the existence of the invisible 'brabos'. All around us were huts, shelters, mats, remains of fires, arrowheads, marked trees and animal traps. These were signs of life I recognised, practices I had learned about during the years I lived with the Xingu peoples of Brazil.

But something new caught my attention: sharp bamboo stakes planted in the ground. Several stakes, camouflaged by leaves – dangerous weapons for the incautious. These were the signs of a people who were resisting fiercely the advances of our society. They were fighting to keep hold of the land that had always been their home.

During the 1970s, the military governments in Brazil started to develop a road network that would cut through the Amazon, destroying the territories of the Indians. Until then, the area had been considered unoccupied, empty. The Government called in many 'sertanistas' to contact the Indians who lay in the way of the road. I was one of them; I was sent out to explore almost unknown areas of forest, leading expeditions with the aim of 'pacifying' isolated tribes. In the years that followed, I stood alongside the Indians as they fought at hydroelectric construction sites, campaigned against oil-prospecting – all in protest against the stealing of their lands. I learned to patch up Indians who were badly wounded from these conflicts. I learned what measles meant to recently contacted tribes – annihilation of their people. And I witnessed Indians losing their identity, their languages and their land.

I began to realise that contact with the outside world is disastrous for uncontacted Indians; once you make contact you start to destroy their universe. And so I began to fight to change long-held policies to those of non-contact; I began to persuade those in power that the state has a duty to protect people – dying remnants of societies that once numbered thousands – who are unable to defend themselves against a much more powerful society.

My beliefs remain as strong today. When a people is isolated and at peace; when nothing threatens them, why do we need to contact them? Just because we know they exist? They very often make it clear that they seek their isolation, so the best thing we can do is stay out of their lives. The first right of isolated peoples is to allow them to remain isolated. And the longer Indian groups can remain uncontacted, the more time we have to rethink the rights of Indians to health, peace, freedom – in short, the right to happiness. The societies which can create aeroplanes and rockets need to develop ideals which truly respect uncontacted Indians. Will the world now accord the last remaining groups their right to freedom? Can we prevent our vast paraphernalia of technology from wrecking their environments? If there is contact in the future, will we be more brotherly, more human, less violent?

———

Sydney Possuelo, Brazil

One day we saw a beetle flying over the top of our house. It was a very big beetle carrying a lot of people. But they were not like us, they were a different people. It was a very big beetle which had arrived to dominate us.

Orlando Makuxi, Brazil

After leaving school, I was lucky enough to be able to travel far and wide. I saw many injustices inflicted on different people in the name of 'progress' and 'development'. Mining, logging, big dams, plantations and road-building projects mean the loss of lands and homes, the loss of knowledge and of beautiful cultures, the death of forests and wildlife.

For most countries, the development model has been the same, regardless of the local conditions. They have taken on vast loans to pay for development infrastructure, and they have sold off natural assets such as trees and minerals to pay for it. Once these are gone, they have nothing left to sell but their intensively grown produce. They then find themselves at the mercy of fluctuating global commodity markets.

For some it has brought prosperity, but for a great many, including tribal peoples, it has brought misery. For tribal peoples to have a chance of survival, we must listen to them, rather than dictate what we think they need. We need to hear their own understanding of development and progress, instead of imposing a one-size fits all formula. We need to pause and really consider what we mean when we talk of 'progress'.

———

Zac Goldsmith, UK

Outsiders who come here always claim they are bringing progress. But all they bring are empty promises. What we're really struggling for is our land. Above all else this is what we need.

———

Arau, Penan, Malaysia

It's not about preserving tribal peoples' pasts. It is very much about their future and their children's future and that of their children's children.

Tribal peoples survive in those parts of the world which, until now, we have not wanted for ourselves. It is inconceivable that our own industrialised society can in any way be threatened by tribal peoples' way of life. Yet they are constantly under threat from ours, and our readiness to destroy them if we find them inconvenient.

If we fail to recognise their rights then by what token do we lay claim to our own? If human rights are simply the preserve of the rich and powerful, then frankly the legacy we leave behind is a miserable one.

—

Colin Firth, UK

I am a red man. If the Great Spirit had wanted me to be a white man, he would have made me so in the first place. It is not necessary for eagles to be crows.

—

Sitting Bull, Hunkpapa Sioux, USA

We are not relics. We are of the here and now.

—

Cherokee Declaration, USA

Our struggle will be over when we have, in our own way, found our place among the many peoples of the earth. And when that time comes, we will still be a people identifiable and independent and proud... Your culture is not the culture of your ancestors of one or 500 years ago. Nor is ours. Our culture is creative. We are developing a twenty-first century culture. And it is and will be an Indian culture.

—

David Courchene, Manitoba, Canada

The day we die a soft breeze
will wipe out our footprints
in the sand.

When the wind dies down,
who will tell in the
timelessness,

That once we walked this
way in the dawn of time?

—
Bushman, Botswana

Pages 66–67
Mongolian Nomads erecting a *ger*
[yurt], Gobi desert, Mongolia
© Cat Vinton /
www.catvphotography.co.uk

Pages 70–71
Penan community, Sarawak,
Malaysia © Andy & Nick Rain /
nickrainphoto@yahoo.co.uk

Page 72
Yanomami yano, Brazil
© Victor Englebert /
www.victorenglebert.com

Page 73
Yanomami yano, Brazil
© Raymond Depardon / Magnum
Photos / www.magnumphotos.com

Pages 74–75
Yanomami, Brazil © Raymond
Depardon / Magnum Photos /
www.magnumphotos.com

Page 76
House at the top of a banyan
tree, Tanna Island, Vanuatu
© Eric Lafforgue /
www.ericlafforgue.com

Page 77
Bushmen hunters resting in the
trunk of a baobab tree, Namibia
© Gideon Mendel /
www.gideonmendel.com

Pages 80–81
Dolgan nomads travelling to a
new camp in their *balok*, a small
wooden hut on runners, Sakha
Republic, Anabar District, Siberia
© Livia Monami /
www.liviamonami.com

Pages 83
Ba'Aka 'Pygmies', Democratic
Republic of the Congo
© Kate Eshelby /
www.kateeshelby.com

Page 84
Penan man, Sarawak,
Malaysia
© Andy & Nick Rain /
nickrainphoto@yahoo.co.uk

Page 85
Penan hunter, Sarawak,
Malaysia
© Andy & Nick Rain /
nickrainphoto@yahoo.co.uk

Page 87
Dongria Kondh women, Orissa,
India
© Jason Taylor /
www.jason-taylor.net

Pages 88–89
Jarawa, Andaman Islands
© Thierry Falise /
www.thierryfalise.com

Page 89
Ashaninka Indians, Brazil
© Mike Goldwater /
www.mikegoldwater.com

Pages 90–91
A kabang, home of Moken
'Sea Gypsies', Mergui
Archipelago, Andaman Sea
© Cat Vinton /
www.catvphotography.co.uk

Pages 118–119
Yanomami shaman, Catrimani
river basin, Brazil
© Claudia Andujar /
cl.andujar@uol.com.br

———

Page 122–123
Yanomami shaman, Catrimani
river basin, Brazil
© Claudia Andujar /
cl.andujar@uol.com.br

———

Pages 124–125
Arhuaco *mamos* [shaman],
Colombia © Yesid Campos /
www.survival-international.org

———

Page 125
Kogi, Colombia © Juan Mayr /
www.survival-international.org

———

Page 126
Kampa (Asháninka) man, Brazil
© Mirella Ricciardi /
www.mirellaricciardi.com /
www.michaelhoppengallery.com

———

Page 127
Envira River, Brazil
© Mike Goldwater /
www.mikegoldwater.com

———

Pages 128–129
Himba women dancing, Namibia
© Adam Hinton /
www.adamhinton.net

———

Page 132
Tree sacred to the Even, Republic
of Sakha, Russia © Livia Monami
/ www.liviamonami.com

———

Page 133
Tsaatan shaman matriach,
Mongolia © Hamid Sardar /
Corbis / www.corbis.com

———

Page 134
A Papuan New Guinean shaman
calls sharks to his canoe, Kontu,
New Ireland, Papua New Guinea
© Chris Rainier /
www.chrisrainier.com

———

Page 135
Siberian shaman prepares a fire
before prayer, Tuva, Russia
© Oleg Klimov

———

Page 136
Barabaig elder, Tanzania
© Charles Lane /
www.survival-international.org

———

Page 137
Night sky, Namibia
© Alex Edwards / Natural High /
www.naturalhighsafaris.com

———

Pages 138–139
Yanomami shaman, Catrimani
river basin, Brazil
© Claudia Andujar /
cl.andujar@uol.com.br

Pages 140–141
Karo woman, Omo river,
Ethiopia
© Eric Lafforgue /
www.ericlafforgue.com

——

Page 145
Yali men and boys, Sibi Valley,
West Papua
© William Milliken /
w.milliken@kew.org

——

Pages 146–147
A Bushman child in a summer
thunderstorm, Makuri, Namibia
© Gideon Mendel /
www.gideonmendel.com

——

Pages 150–151
Bushmen of the Kalahari,
Namibia © Brent Stirton /
www.brentstirton.com

——

Page 153
Yanomami man making an arrow,
Toototobi river, Brazil
© Victor Englebert /
www.victorenglebert.com

——

Pages 156–157
Yanomami hunter, Catrimani
river basin, Brazil

© Claudia Andujar /
cl.andujar@uol.com.br

——

Page 159
Three generations of women,
Tibet
© Caroline Halley des Fontaines /
www.carolinehalley.com

——

Pages 160–161
Hmong women, Vietnam
© Dieter Telemans / Panos
Pictures/www.panos.co.uk

Pages 190–191
Maasai hunters, Kenya
© Caroline Halley des Fontaines /
www.carolinehalley.com

Page 195
Tarahumara man, Mexico
© John Running /
www.johnrunning.com

Pages 196–197
Guarani children, Brazil
© João Ripper /
www.survival-international.org

Page 197
Yanomami father and son,
Toototobi river, Brazil
© Victor Englebert /
www.victorenglebert.com

Page 198
Aborigine child, Coonana,
Australia
© Alastair McNaughton /
www.desertimages.com.au

Page 200
Karo man, Omo Valley, Ethiopia
© Eric Lafforgue /
www.ericlafforgue.com

Page 201
Hamar woman, Omo Valley,
Ethiopia
© Eric Lafforgue /
www.ericlafforgue.com

Pages 202–203
Papuan woman at a festival,
Mount Hagen, Papua
© Eric Lafforgue /
www.ericlafforgue.com

Page 205
Uncontacted Indians seen from the
air, May 2008, Acre State, Brazil
© Gleison Miranda / FUNAI

Page 206
Guarani preparing to re-occupy
their land, Brazil
© Simon Rawles /
www.simonrawles.co.uk

Page 207
Penan family, Sarawak,
Malaysia
© Andy & Nick Rain /
nickrainphoto@yahoo.co.uk

Page 208
Asháninka mother and child,
Acre, Brazil

© Mike Goldwater /
www.mikegoldwater.com

Page 209
Asháninka Indian crosses the
river, Acre, Brazil
© Mike Goldwater /
www.mikegoldwater.com

Page 210
Kayabi girl, Brazil
© CIMI

Page 211
Tibetan nomads wait to enter the
Jokhang Temple, Lhasa, Tibet
© Steve McCurry / Magnum
Photos / www.stevemccurry.com

Pages 212–213
Bushmen women walking to
gather roots and berries, Kalahari
Desert, Botswana
© Sebastião Salgado /
www.amazonasimages.com

Page 223
Himba village enclosure, Kunene
region, Namibia
© Yann Arthus-Bertrand /
www.yannarthusbertrand.org

Page 224
Moken child, Surin Islands,
Thailand
© Andrew Testa /
www.andrewtesta.co.uk

Publisher's acknowledgements

The publisher has made every effort to trace the copyright holders of the text extracts quoted within this book. We apologise in advance for any unintentional omission and would be pleased to insert the appropriate acknowledgement in any subsequent edition of this book.

PAGE 14 Reproduced by permission of The University of Nebraska Press from *Land of the Spotted Eagle* by Luther Standing Bear. Copyright © Luther Standing Bear. All rights reserved.

PAGE 18 Reproduced by permission of The Random House Group Ltd from *The Lost World of the Kalahari* by Laurens van der Post, published by Chatto & Windus. Copyright © Laurens van der Post. All rights reserved.

PAGE 38 Reproduced by permission of HarperPerennial from *The Reindeer People: Living with Animals and Spirits in Siberia* by Piers Vitebsky. Copyright © Piers Vitebsky. All rights reserved.

PAGE 49 Courtesy of Jacques Ivanoff.

PAGE 55 Reproduced by permission of Faber and Faber from *The Other Side of Eden: Hunter-gatherers, Farmers and the Shaping of the World* by Hugh Brody. Copyright © Hugh Brody. All rights reserved.

PAGE 56 Reproduced by permission of HarperPerennial from *The Reindeer People: Living with Animals and Spirits in Siberia* by Piers Vitebsky. Copyright © Piers Vitebsky. All rights reserved.

PAGE 61 Reproduced by permission of HarperCollins from *Under the Mountain Wall* by Peter Matthiessen, published by Harvill, an imprint of HarperCollins. Copyright © Peter Matthiessen. All rights reserved.

PAGE 63 Reproduced by permission of Profile Books from *In Search of Kazakhstan: The Land That Disappeared* by Christopher Robbins, published by Profile Books, 2007. Copyright © Christopher Robbins, 2007. All rights reserved.

PAGE 80 Reproduced by permission of HarperPerennial from *The Reindeer People: Living with Animals and Spirits in Siberia* by Piers Vitebsky. Copyright © Piers Vitebsky. All rights reserved.

PAGE 90 Courtesy of Jacques Ivanoff.

PAGE 98 Reproduced by permission of Penguin from *Tribe: Adventures in a Changing World* by Bruce Parry, published by Michael Joseph, 2007, 2008. Copyright © Endeavour Productions Ltd, 2007. All rights reserved.

PAGE 104 Reproduced by permission of Macmillan from *No Man's Land: An Investigative Journey Through Kenya and Tanzania* by George Monbiot, published by Picador. Copyright © George Monbiot. All rights reserved.

PAGE 106 Reproduced by permission of HarperCollins from *Maasai* by Tepilit Ole Saitoti and Carol Beckwith, published by Harvill, an imprint of HarperCollins. Copyright © 2009. All rights reserved.

PAGE 108–109 Reproduced by permission of The Random House Group Ltd from *The Lost World of the Kalahari* by Laurens van der Post, published by Chatto & Windus. Copyright © Laurens van der Post. All rights reserved.

PAGE 113 Reproduced by permission of D&M Publishers Inc. from *Inuksuit: Silent Messengers of the Arctic* by Norman Hallendy, published by Douglas & McIntyre, 2000, a division of D&M Publishers Inc. Copyright © Norman Hallendy, 2000. All rights reserved.

PAGE 126 Reproduced by permission of Penguin from *Shamanic Voices: A Survey of Visionary Narratives* by Joan Halifax, published by Penguin. Copyright © Joan Halifax, 1991. All rights reserved.

PAGE 133 Reproduced by permission of The Random House Group Ltd from *In Siberia* by Colin Thubron, published by Chatto & Windus. Copyright © Colin Thubron, 1999. All rights reserved.

PAGE 135 Reproduced by permission of Penguin from *Shamanic Voices: A Survey of Visionary Narratives* by Joan Halifax, published by Penguin. Copyright © Joan Halifax, 1991. All rights reserved.

PAGE 136 Reproduced by permission of Macmillan from *No Man's Land: An Investigative Journey Through Kenya and Tanzania* by George Monbiot. Copyright © George Monbiot. All rights reserved.

PAGE 184 Reprinted with the permission of Scribner, a Divison of Simon & Schuster, Inc., from *Custer Died for Your Sins: An Indian Manifesto* by Vine Deloria Jr. Copyright © 1969 by Vine Deloria Jr. Copyright renewed © 1997 by Vine Deloria Jr. All rights reserved.

Editor's acknowledgements

We Are One is a true collaboration and many people have helped me during its creation. In addition to the worldwide contributors who have so readily and generously donated their words and images to the book, I would like to express my thanks to Robin Hanbury-Tenison and Stephen Corry who supported my idea for *We Are One* from the beginning and have inspired me throughout.

Also for their help and support in various ways, I would like to thank the following: the wonderful team at Survival International, James Barry, Jonny Baynes, Julia Borispolets, Alan Campbell, Lucy and Justin Eede, Natascha Lloyd, Beatrice Newbery, Elizabeth Orange, Harry Ram, Kate Rew and Araminta Whitley. Also the staff at Quadrille Publishing, Anne Furniss, Lisa Pendreigh, Lawrence Morton and Ruth Deary. Many thanks also go to Marinda Solari-Lavut, who joined the *We Are One* team at just the right moment and who instinctively understood the philosophy of the book, and also to Clare Brookman of Survival International, for her photographic memory, unflagging enthusiasm and ideas. In particular my grateful thanks to my parents, John and Judith Eede, who read and reread *We Are One* over the course of several months, for their research, observations and endless good humour. Finally, with love to Agatha, my newborn niece.

Creator and Editor Joanna Eede
Editorial Director Anne Furniss
Creative Director Helen Lewis
Project Editor Lisa Pendreigh
Art Director and Designer Lawrence Morton
Picture Researchers Joanna Eede and Clare Brookman
Picture Assistant Katherine Cordwell
Editorial Assistants Sarah Jones and Marinda Solari-Lavut
Production Director Vincent Smith
Production Controller Ruth Deary

First published in 2009 by
Quadrille Publishing Ltd
Alhambra House
27–31 Charing Cross Road
London WC2H 0LS
www.quadrille.co.uk

Text © see page 222

Design and layout © 2009
Quadrille Publishing Ltd

British Library Cataloguing-in-Publication Data
A catalogue record for this book is available from the British Library.

ISBN 978 184400 729 5

Printed in China

You have seen with your eyes what is happening here.
Go and tell people what you have seen.
We need more international support so we can have the rights to our land.
What would make us happy is if we have the rights to stay on our land.

Ramarari Tshotlego, Bushman, Botswana